BRIGHT IDEAS

Inspirations

for S...

& LI...

1wk loan

This book is to be returned on or before
the last date stamped below.

4·3·02
7·11·02

18-11-02
27·11·02
6·12-02
6·· 01·03

13·10·03
31·01·03

3 0 NOV 2009

D0309824

Published by Scholastic
Publications Ltd,
Villiers House,
Clarendon Avenue,
Leamington Spa,
Warwickshire CV32 5PR

© 1992 Scholastic Publications Ltd

Written by Alistair Ross
Edited by Juliet Gladston
Sub-edited by Catherine Baker
Series designed by Juanita
Puddifoot
Illustrated by Conny Jude
Cover design by Clare Brewer
Cover artwork by Jeff Cummins

Designed using Aldus Pagemaker
Processed by Pages Bureau,
Leamington Spa
Printed in Great Britain by
Ebenezer Baylis & Son, Worcester

**British Library Cataloguing in
Publication Data**
A catalogue record for this book is
available from the British Library.

ISBN 0-590-53016-X

CONTENTS

Speaking and listening

Talking and listening come naturally to all but a very small minority of children. They normally begin to acquire speech in the home, before schooling starts, and recent studies have shown both what a rich experience the home provides, and what powerful learning takes place when children and parents talk together (Wells, G. [1987] The Meaning Makers, *Hodder & Stoughton*; and Tizard, B. and Hughes, M. [1984] Young Children Learning, Talking and Thinking at Home and at School, *Fontana*).

So why should teachers be concerned to provide opportunities in school for what, after all, comes naturally? Many primary teachers, up until fairly recently, would have said that their children were only too practised at talking, and instead needed to learn to be quiet in order to get on with the real work of the school. However, there have been major changes in our understanding of how children use language in their learning – all their learning and not just their language learning – and this has led to an increasing emphasis on children developing their oracy skills throughout their schooling and not just in the very early years.

BACKGROUND

The development of oral skills is becoming recognised as a more complex process than had once been thought: more complex for the child, as a learner, and more complex for the teacher. As teachers, we need to make fine judgements about the timing and nature of our interventions into children's talk. Most of our own communication with children is through talk, and through this talk we provide both role-models for children and a structured environment for their talk.

This book explores the ways in which children can develop their skills of speaking and listening. It suggests ideas for activities that are real for children, as opposed to exercises divorced from the everyday use of language.

Why talk? Why listen?

The obvious value of oral language is as a means of communication. While we can – and do – also communicate through media such as gesture, number and art, language has special qualities of exactitude, range and expression that make it essential for everyday life. Oral language has a particularly vital place as it is more widely used than both the written and read modes of language. It also has an important social role, which has been accentuated by the growth of technologies such as the telephone and television.

It is thought that most young adults have a vocabulary of some 100,000 words. If these were learned at a steady rate, it would mean that children would be acquiring some twenty new words a day throughout their years of schooling (although in reality the rate of learning may be higher in the primary years than later). Most of this

It goes through this one because it's got a hole!

vocabulary will be used in an oral context, rather than written or read. However, there is more to speaking and listening in the primary school than acquiring a wide vocabulary and developing the skills of oral communication. Speaking and listening have an essential role in the ways in which we learn.

Speaking and listening to learn

Learning is a social activity: what we are taught is socially determined and our understanding of it is acquired through social intercourse. Our curriculum is constructed by society and it is us, and other people like us, who determine what knowledge is, how it should be classified and why it is sufficiently important to be transmitted to future

generations. We learn by exchanging and refining descriptions of our experiences. In talking, we explore, experiment, rehearse and investigate the meaning of words. We invest words with layers of abstraction that turn them into concepts which allow us to analyse our environment. In all these activities conversation, argument, interrogation, description and discussion are crucial elements. Oral language is a necessary part of the way in which nearly everyone thinks and orders their understanding.

But how do children do this? One approach, that has become an established tradition in primary schools, is

to encourage children to discover for themselves, as was advocated in the Plowden Report of 1967, *Children and their Primary Schools* (Central Advisory Council on Education [England], HMSO). Teacher intervention was regarded as potentially dangerous and Jean Piaget warned 'each time one prematurely teaches a child something [he] could have discovered [himself], the child is kept from inventing it and consequently from understanding it completely [sic]' (quoted in Edwards, D. and Mercer, N. [1987] *Common Knowledge: the Development of*

Understanding in the Classroom, Methuen).

However, language is only meaningful if it is a shared medium. We need to have perceptions that are similar to the perceptions of other people if we are to understand the word 'chaos', for example, or the expression 'Have a nice day'.

A conflict of interests

Besides discovery and understanding, education is also about introducing an existing shared culture and knowledge to children. What has happened in many classrooms is that teachers have been torn between two separate needs of the children; to develop their individual understanding and to introduce them to a shared acceptance of meaning. This can be seen in much teacher-talk in the classroom, where the teacher questions the child or a group of children in what appears to be an open way, but is in reality a way of asking the child to search for the 'right' answer. This then simply becomes a game of guessing what is in the teacher's mind, a form of interaction described as the 'initiation (I)–response (R)–feedback (F)' framework (Sinclair, J. and Coulthard, M. [1975] *Towards an Analysis of Discourse*, Oxford University Press).

The following example of this type of interaction shows what can happen when a child's guesses do not match the teacher's expectations.

Here the teacher begins by asking how a diagram on the blackboard, showing a route map of cities and motorway links, could be communicated to a person in the next room.

Child: Morse Code. (R)
Teacher: Morse Code, well that is not necessary. We can speak to him – he is only on the other side of the door. If I was to put you on the other side of the door, you could hear what I was saying. (F)
Child: Co-ordinates. (R)
Teacher: Co-ordinates would be one way of doing it. That would be a very good way of doing it. What do you mean by co-ordinates? (F, then I)
Child: Say five across and down this way. (R)
Teacher: Well, that is a very good idea, it is one I certainly had not thought of. Any other bright ideas? (F, then I)
Child: Hold up a mirror. (R)
Teacher: Hold up a mirror – it cannot go through a solid door. (R)

(This passage is taken from Yates, J. [1978] 'Four Mathematic Classrooms', University of Southampton, quoted in D. Pimm [1990] *Speaking Mathematically*, Routledge.)

The teacher in this extract controls the dialogue, not just formally, but also in requiring the 'correct' answer. The answer 'co-ordinates' is a perfectly sensible suggestion, but it is not the one that the teacher had in mind and is therefore incorrect. The rules that govern this sort of exchange have been described by Edwards and Mercer (1987) as:

• The teacher asks the question.
• The teacher knows the answer.
• Repeated questions mean the wrong answer was given.
(Edwards, D. and Mercer, N. [1987] *Common Knowledge:*

The Development of Understanding in the Classroom, Methuen.)

Contrast this with another example shown below. Here the teacher is chairing a discussion between a class of Year 6 children and a factory worker called Dot. The teacher wants the children to explore the question: 'Is it possible for women to perform the skilled engineering roles in the tool-room?'

Ian: ...we thought ladies probably couldn't work in the tool room, 'cos it would be too hard for them.... I mean, men are – you know – more tougher, and they know how to – like, you know, engineers, mechanically repairing things – but ladies, you know....

Teacher: Does anyone in the group want to say anything about that first of all, before we come back to Dot? Sula?
Sula: When Ian said that – what about if a woman can do that job in the tool room, like....
Teacher: ...yes, do you think she can do it?
Sula: No, sir, can I just say this?
Teacher: Yes, OK.
Sula: What if a woman could do that job, she'd been trained and had experience, and she went to the managing director and told him she wanted to work in the tool room, because she knew how to do it – what if

the managing director said she couldn't, although she [was able to] do it?
(This passage is taken from Ross, A. [1983], 'The Bottle Stopper Factory: Talking Altogether', *The English Magazine* 11 [Summer].)

Here the teacher negotiates with the child, and is able to accept that the child could construct a valid alternative question. The differences between the two examples lie partly in intention – in the first example, the teacher's purpose is unambiguous, in that he wants the children to recognise a 'useful' context for map work, while in the second example, the teacher has the twin aims of developing skills of questioning and exploring gender stereotyping. When this teacher makes his second intervention ('Yes, do you think she can do it?') he is steering towards the discussion of gender; but a moment later ('Yes, OK') he has abandoned this in favour of letting Sula try out her own question. In the end, the teacher's decision is rewarded: Sula makes her point about gender restrictions at work in her own words.

In both examples, however, there is a tension between the teachers' desires to let the children seem to take the initiative, to be responsible for discovery, and the teachers' responsibilities, to have the children construct some socially agreed and accepted version of reality (maps can be described and used to convey information; we can look critically at how other people think men and women have different work roles).

What is the answer to this seeming conflict of interests? And what role does talk play in this? Vygotsky suggested that young children begin by using language as a means of social interaction and then, later, internalise the meanings of language to make and modify their mental map of the world around them (Vygotsky, L. [1962] *Thought and Language*, Wiley). Piaget's model was of the child alone, learning as an individual by actively exploring the physical world (Piaget, J. and Inhelder, B. [1969] *The Psychology of the Child*, Routledge). However, Vygotsky suggested language was the main source of intellectual development; in other words, the child talks with adults and peers to arrive at a shared, joint construction of the world (Vygotsky, 1962).

Bruner described the teacher's task as using language to erect the 'scaffolding' for learning, a verbal framework that allows the child to develop

independence (Bruner, J. [1983] *Child's Talk: Learning to use Language*, Oxford University Press). However, not giving children the space to interact with each other, to hang ideas on the scaffolding or to negotiate and jointly construct meanings, leads to children being unable to internalise the knowledge that the teacher intends them to learn.

One solution is to make the purpose of the learning explicit. In the first of the examples quoted above, the teacher need not have played the guessing game, but could have announced that the purpose of the exercise was to explore how mapping could be used as one of the ways to pass information to the person in the next room. In the second example (although one of the purposes was different: how to develop useful interrogatory skills that elicit the information needed), the teacher could have framed the question for Sula in a way that directed her towards gender roles. In the first example, the children were left guessing about the purpose of the activity and the knowledge that they were intended to acquire. ('It's not co-ordinates so let's try mirrors.') In the second example, the child knows that the teacher has his own agenda, but feels confident enough to challenge this, and to ask if she can make her point. A child-centred ideology can result in teachers feeling that they will restrict children's learning if they make their aims too explicit, and failing to understand that meaning is jointly constructed between children and teacher.

This crucial interaction between thinking, acting and verbalising is developed by David Wood (1988) in *How Children Think and Learn* (Blackwell). He argues that what some children lack 'is not "language" as such, but experience in putting it to certain uses'.

The bilingual child

Children whose home or community language is not English will need to develop the same skills of talking and listening as their English-only speaking counterparts. Oral skills will almost invariably be the way in which they begin to achieve competence in English,

so talking and listening skills will be particularly important for them. Much of the spoken English which they will encounter will be from their peers – for example, in the playground – and this can be extended by bringing them fully into oral work done in the classroom. From oral work written and reading forms will soon emerge.

The major task for the teachers of bilingual children must be to bathe them in language. This should not be limited to interaction with the teacher, but should involve talking with other children in the class, who can contribute so much more in terms of available time. The language that the child hears should be as natural as possible, at a level and vocabulary appropriate to the age and development of the child, rather than to her stage of English language development. Children will learn much better using the current language of

their peers than through being confined to the language used by much younger children.

It is also important to help them, wherever possible, to feel confident about using and maintaining their own spoken (and written) community language: bilingualism is an attribute much sought after and valued in adult life and it is a waste to allow such children to lose this skill while still at school. It can also be a way in which you can stress the ability and competence of a child who may feel himself to be struggling alongside children who are already fluent English speakers. Stressing their skills, letting them use their community language to interpret and help other bilingual learners, all this can raise the self-esteem of the English language learner.

Dialect, accent and standard English

All English is spoken in some sort of dialect: even 'standard', 'received' or 'BBC' English is only another form of dialect. Most adults, and indeed most children, use two or more dialects, switching from one register to another according to the context in which they find themselves. On occasions, a non-standard accent is appropriate or even necessary – imagine rap delivered in received pronunciation!

One of the skills of teaching oral skills in primary schools is to encourage children to develop a sense of context, so that they are able to operate in the accent and dialect that is appropriate. This is a delicate business, for even a mildly censorious attitude towards the dialect of the child or her home may result in her retreating from using – and developing – her oral skills in school.

Monitoring talk

Speaking and listening allow us to communicate with others, and to develop understanding with others. But for speaking and listening to be successful in the classroom, the teacher must have considerable faith and confidence in the children in his class. Talking is necessarily not a quiet activity, and sometimes it needs to be downright noisy. Talking is very often not directed towards the teacher, but to other children, in pairs and in groups, and therefore you cannot expect to monitor all the talk that is going on in the classroom. Clearly, some of the talking will be with you and here you will be able to exercise more control. But you can only ever hope to sample

the rest of the talk that's going on in the classroom – to listen in, where appropriate, and sometimes to tape-record, with the children's assent. This is not abdicating your role as teacher: it is giving children the space and the time in which to develop and refine their linguistic skills, within the parameters and guidance that you lay down.

Clearly, you will try to ensure that most talk is 'on-task', but some talk will, almost inevitably, not be. This doesn't mean that it is of less value: all speaking and listening is communication with others, and can help to develop understanding of others.

How to use this book

This book develops various ideas about the importance of oral language. Each of the first

six chapters takes as its theme one of a variety of modes in which speaking and listening take place. Each mode is introduced with a brief analysis of the key points in developing the necessary competencies in speaking and listening. There are also ideas for the practical classroom organisation that is essential if children are to learn.

The final four chapters introduce some of the contexts and arenas for using oral skills, though clearly every area of the curriculum can – and should – involve the use of high-level speaking and listening skills.

Within each chapter are a series of activities. While many of these can be attempted as one-offs, they will be more effective if used in the broader context suggested in the

introductory section of each chapter. It is there that the rationale for the activities is explained, and suggestions given for the sequence in which activities can be tackled in order to maximise the development of skills and understanding.

Each activity is laid out to give:
• an idea of the age range for which it is suitable – though many can be adapted fairly easily for younger or older children or even for adults;
• an indication of the size of group in which the activity might be conducted;
• a list of materials that need to be prepared before the activity can be started;
• a short description of how to introduce the activity, indicating where appropriate the kind of responses that you might get and the sorts of questions that you might pose;
• suggestions for work that might follow on from the main activity – either for all the group, to enhance their skills, or for those who complete the activity faster.

Messengers and planners

One of the most straightforward ways in which children speak and listen is through messages. Passing on ideas and making information clear are important early stages in planning what to do, and Chapter 1 covers how to develop oral skills as the children co-operate to plan events in a variety of curriculum areas.

Reporters

When speakers move on to become reporters, they do more than simply pass on a message or a description. They put their information into an order and they decide what to include and what to leave out. This means that they have to consider their listeners as an audience. Who are they? What do they already know? What do they need to hear and in what order? Equally, the audience need to consider those who are reporting: are they giving a complete and accurate account?

Instructors

Telling someone what to do calls for a particularly clear and logical way of speaking. Chapter 3 describes how children can build up a clarity of analysis and expression in giving directions to others. These activities involve a variety of curricular areas.

Story-tellers

Telling tales opens up a world of imagination and excitement. Chapter 4 explores a variety of contexts in which stories can be developed, refined and presented, and looks at ways in which particular elements of the oral story can be developed by children.

Discussions

The first four chapters presuppose a fairly simple speaker-listener relationship. Discussions, however, introduce a set of more complex roles, in which children need to negotiate, through oral give-and-take, ideas and viewpoints and an order of speaking. This crucial chapter shows how even young children can begin to develop sophisticated skills of managing a discussion. A variety of introductory activities lead small groups to build up strategies that allow them to interact with each other in a constructive and collaborative manner.

Interviewers

Getting information from other people is not a simple matter of asking questions. Activities in chapter 6 develop techniques of interacting with those being interviewed: of listening to what is being said and of responding to it. Talking with adults other than teachers is a very useful way of helping children to understand the way in which people work together. Children need to become aware of the needs and the viewpoints of other people and this calls for the development of particular skills of investigation.

Talking about the past

Exploring the past through talking to people who have lived through it, is an important way to develop historical skills, both in investigating the recent past and in local history. Chapter 7 shows how children can begin to work with older visitors to the classroom: how they can help people to recall the past, assess memories and compare oral accounts with other sources.

Talking mathematics

While mathematics works through a language of its own, it is also made explicit and given a context in spoken language. Meaning can often be obscured in this translation between the numbers and icons of mathematics and the words and phrases of everyday speech. Chapter 8 looks at some of the ways of keeping the meaning when talking about mathematics.

It's only make believe

Chapter 9 provides a collection of fantasy locations and everyday stimuli to encourage children to narrate. It suggests a range of experiences and sensations to fire the imagination.

Imaginary worlds

Role-play is one of the ways in which children's talk begins to flow. This final activity chapter suggests a range of ways in which children can develop roles, and focuses on the variety of language opportunities provided by creating different locations.

Recording and assessing progress

There are no simple ways of assessing children's development in speaking and listening skills. Much of what children say is, quite properly, to each other, and teachers do not hear it. But there are ways of noting progress that do not depend on time-consuming monitoring of everything that children say. Teachers also need to keep simple records of the variety of speaking that is going on in the class, in groups and by individual children. Chapter 11 outlines some practical ideas.

Resources

Ideas about speaking and listening in the classroom have generated quite a quantity of written material. Chapter 12 suggests some of the publications that you might go on to read – both to develop a greater theoretical understanding of children's development of oracy, and to get more practical ideas of possible classroom activities. It also provides a brief guide to equipment that might prove useful.

Teaching guide with attainment targets

Chapter 13 covers the National Curriculum statements of attainment and programmes of study relating to speaking and

listening, together with a quick-reference guide to the activities in this book which support them.

Photocopiable pages

Some of these photocopiable pages cover record-keeping and assessment, while others can be used to stimulate oral work with children. They range from forms and charts that can be filled in by you or the children, to settings for simulations. You are free to photocopy all these sheets and to adapt them to meet your own particular requirements.

CHAPTER 1

Messengers and planners

In the development of human language, speech came first, as a simple and direct method of face-to-face communication. It would have been associated with gestures and body language to make meaning clearer.

The limitations of oral language are clear. More complex organisation, keeping records and communicating at a distance have all become easier with the development of other communication systems such as writing. Gradually over the centuries, print took over many of the functions of speech, though of course, direct speech has always been used for many communications.

More recently still, we have developed other forms of communication that reassert the primacy of speech as a communicative medium. But now our technologies allow us to use speech away from the face-to-face context. Telephones, television and broadcasting, tape recorders and video-recorders require powerful skills of speaking and listening if they are to be used effectively.

BACKGROUND

Using speaking and listening to plan and to carry messages may seem obvious, but the skills involved need to be developed throughout the primary school years. Children need to be given space in which to develop their oral language and listening skills – physical space and space within the school day. They need to be able to use simple equipment that involves speaking and listening. They need to develop techniques that enable them to make speaking and listening work for them. This chapter begins to develop ways of meeting these needs.

Physical requirements

Talking and listening are made easier if a number of simple physical requirements are met. It is much easier to hear and understand what someone else is saying if you are facing the speaker and can see and interpret her facial expression and body language, as well as simply hear the words she says. Of course, this is somewhat easier if there are few sounds competing with the voice you are listening to. It is remarkable how one can follow a particular voice in a hubbub of conversations – but for children in a classroom context, competing noises may be more attractive! Therefore, if at all possible, try to organise listening and talking activities in a relatively quiet area where the children involved can easily see each other's faces.

However, in a busy and at times cramped classroom, this may not be easy to arrange. Quiet corners or a carpeted area can often provide suitable sites for talk. Audio equipment can be located at the opposite side of the room to the construction or technology area (though this is not to suggest that technology work doesn't also require a great deal of talking and listening). For a class discussion (see Chapter 5), chairs can be arranged so that children sit in a circle, facing each other. Some talk might be more appropriate, convenient or

successful if it were conducted outside in the corridor or in the library.

Time

Different kinds of talk will need different locations and will take place at different times in the day or week. This can, to an extent, be planned as you organise your teaching. When do you have space and time to chat with individual children in the class? How do you ensure that you will be able to talk in this way with members of the class? As a junior teacher, I often found time for this when walking from the class to the library or to the games field.

You also need to consider when discussions between groups of children will take place. How can learning activities in science, technology, history or maths be devised so that they allow children to collaborate in exploring ideas? Collaboration means talking and listening, and collaboration is an essential part of how we learn because it is the time at which nascent ideas are formulated and exchanged. Therefore, the planning for many kinds of learning needs to include time for appropriate kinds of conversation, whether between children or between teacher and children.

The activities in this chapter suggest ways in which a class can work together to develop their listening and speaking skills. Some of the activities are exercises or games in which talk is perhaps rather artificially induced. These activities are a means to an end. They are suggested as ways of getting children to begin to modify their oral behaviour in the classroom, and can be dropped as soon as the quality of talking and listening begins to improve.

Other activities are organisational ploys: ways of getting children to reflect upon the ways in which they speak and organise their talk. Some of these activities are also artificial, in that they set up formal patterns to share information and network ideas between groups. Nevertheless, they demonstrate to children in a practical way, the usefulness of planning how information is to be shared.

ACTIVITIES

Using equipment

The four activities in this section centre on familiarising the children with everyday audio-visual equipment and using it effectively. The first three activities, in particular, require children to talk and listen in a rather unnatural way, when they cannot see the person with whom they are talking and listening. So as well as familiarising themselves with the equipment, they are also learning to modify their ways of talking in order to communicate more clearly and concisely. It is worth making an effort to familiarise all the children with the telephone, but a particular effort should be made with those children who do not have a phone at home.

1. Tape recorders

Age range
Five to eleven.

Group size
Any size.

What you need
A tape recorder with headsets if available, short tapes (many LEAs and educational suppliers

have five-minute tapes), self-adhesive labels.

What to do
Simply use any available context to encourage the children to leave and receive messages and instructions for each other on tape. One of the objectives of this would be for the children to familiarise themselves as much as possible with using a tape recorder, for example, knowing how to load a tape, checking it is recording and so on.

You could leave messages for groups of children, perhaps setting them a task in maths, or introducing them to some writing or a new game. (This

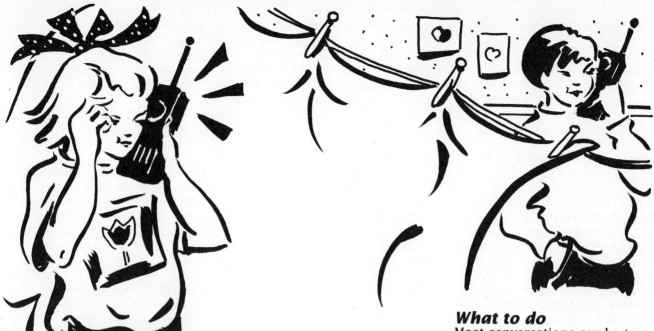

also allows you to work directly with another group at the same time.) The children could then leave you a short comment on their work, or they might want to leave messages for another group.

If you only provide short tapes, this will encourage the children to plan and compose concise messages. Having sticky labels readily available means that each fresh message can be identified, for example:

'From: Susie and David's group.
To: Miss Jenkins.
Date: 2 November.'

Remember that children who are not used to handling tape recorders will need encouragement to check that they are recording messages that are audible.

Using a tape recorder can also be an invaluable way of encouraging shy or reticent children to participate.

Further activity
Think about setting up a quiet corner of the classroom as a recording studio. It needn't be very big – the presenters of children's programmes on the BBC claim to have their studio in a broom cupboard!

2. Walkie-talkie

Age range
Seven to eleven.

Group size
Initially in pairs and then the whole class.

What you need
Either a real walkie-talkie set (a battery operated two-way radio set that is effective over short distances), or two empty tins connected by a taut string.

What to do
Most conversations can be two-way at the same time, with both partners talking and listening at once. We can interrupt the person who's talking to us, intervene, signal that we want to take over the conversation or talk over them. This is even true of telephone conversations, where we can't see the other person and make judgements from their appearance.

An interesting feature of walkie-talkies – whether two-way radios or tins on strings – is that the message can only travel one way at a time, as each person is either transmitting (speaking) or receiving (listening). Working out how to cope with this phenomenon teaches the children to notice and analyse all the complex skills they already possess and use when conducting a 'normal' conversation.

Set up a walkie-talkie system with two children. Ensure that they cannot hear each other directly, and preferably cannot see each other either (you could use a sheet or a

newspaper as a screen). Ask them to use the walkie-talkie for a task that involves planning something; for example they could:
• plan a surprise for another child or for their parents;
• decide on a good place for a school trip;
• make a list of books they'd like to add to the school library.

As they plan they will want to exchange ideas fairly quickly, and will find that they need to develop ways to show when they've finished talking and want a response. With the 'real' walkie-talkie the controls have to be set to transmit or to receive, while with the can-and-string model the users have to decide how to switch. In both cases, the children will discover that they need to signal the end of each of their utterances and to agree a way of ending the whole conversation. They will also discover that it's better to have fairly short utterances, so that the receiver can check what's been said.

Further activity
Discuss with small groups of children how talking on a walkie-talkie is different from an ordinary conversation. Ask them how, in everyday talk, we know when it's our 'turn' to speak, how we check that the listener understands what we are saying and what signals we use to start and end conversations.

3. Phones

Age range
Seven to eleven – although children as young as five will benefit from aspects of this.

Group size
Individuals or pairs.

What you need
Ideally, access in the classroom to a phone connected to an internal switchboard, so that the children can dial and talk with other classrooms at no cost. Otherwise, a phone connected to an external line and a number of willing volunteers outside the school.

What to do
Arrange for all the children to experience making and receiving a phone call. Thirty short incoming local calls and thirty short outgoing calls will cost about the same as a paperback book.

Children also need to know and discuss:
• how and when to dial the emergency service;
• how to contact the operator;
• the costs involved in making phone calls – and particularly the costs of chat lines and the so-called 'premium services'.

Further activities
Discuss with the children the different ways in which we speak on the phone. Older children can also talk about the

social implications of people making nuisance calls. Talk about the possibility of receiving obscene calls and how to deal with them.

4. 'Developing tray'

Age range
Seven to eleven.

Group size
Groups of three to six.

What you need
A microcomputer, a 'developing tray' program (sometimes called *Tray*, *Devtray* or *Wiztray*).

What to do
This type of program is named after the idea of a photographic developing tray, in which the image gradually appears on the paper as it is gently shaken in the developing fluid. In this case, a piece of text gradually appears on a screen as children make guesses about what the words and sentences are.

Typically, the screen will start off showing just a series of dashes for each letter. It's also possible to have some letters in place from the start – generally between 12 and 15 of the least common ones. Children can identify the single letters – usually 'a' or 'i' – and they can type in their ideas for these and other words, and check them. It's best to try to hypothesise about whole chunks of texts – phrases, whole lines, sentences – rather than individual letters.

The program is designed to develop the skills of reading and understanding texts, but it is also a marvellous stimulus for talk. Groups of children will discuss various possibilities, argue about alternatives, point out flaws in each other's suggestions, and come to an agreement on what to check.

Further activity
There are many types of text that you could use, and with each type the children will need to bring and share different experiences that they have had of texts. You could include:

- poems;
- advertisements;
- jokes;
- menus;
- letters;
- newspaper stories.

Each kind of text has its own structure and vocabulary – even its own layout on the page.

Functions of talk

The activities in this section are intended to help the children collaborate in planning activities, developing their talking and listening skills as they initiate activities in a whole series of possible contexts across the curriculum.

As children progress through the primary school, they need to become more autonomous and take an increasing responsibility for

directing their own learning. This is not to abrogate the responsibility of the teacher for what children learn, but to acknowledge that we must allow children to incorporate aspects of their own experiences into the curriculum.

5. Brainstorming

Age range
Five to eleven.

Group size
Small groups or the whole class.

What you need
A large sheet of paper pinned up where everyone can see it, a thick felt-tipped pen.

What to do
This is a classic and well-known technique for generating and sharing ideas. Write the key word or focus phrase in the middle or at the top of the paper. The children should then add ideas as quickly as they can, forming long lists or a spider's web of ideas. The children need to express their thoughts concisely and clearly as they call out their ideas, and to think rapidly about the potentials and problems of each other's ideas.

It is usually best if one person can act as a scribe, though the pen can be shared so that everyone can add ideas as they please. The scribe's role is critical: he must not only be a fluent and clear writer, but must think quickly about where to put ideas on the sheet. It is possible, for example, to write similar kinds of answers together, so that the rest of the group see categories beginning to emerge. It is also possible to

brainstorm from one of the new ideas on the list, exploring it further.

Further activity
Brainstorming is only the start: the group will need to determine which of the many ideas they will develop further. Activity 6 may follow on naturally.

6. Planning events

Age range
Five to eleven (younger children will need help).

Group size
Varies, depending on the context.

What you need
A quiet place to talk, paper and pencils, photocopiable page 176.

What to do
Focus the children's discussion on how they will plan and carry out some group event. It might be making a class magazine, organising a menu for a tea-

party, preparing a wall display or planning some collaborative writing. When developing oral communication skills, the content is less important than the context.

The group will need to make a number of decisions about what is to be done and who will do it. Photocopiable page 176 provides a series of headings around which the group might structure their talk.

The children will need to agree on the purpose of the activity, for example, who they are doing it for, what they want, and when it must be ready by. They will then need to assess their various talents – who is good at what, what can they do well collectively and so on.

Finally, they will need to decide on the order in which things need to be done and whether it is possible for several things to be done at the same time by different people.

This is not really a one-off activity. The children will improve in their ability to organise themselves each time they do something like this, so the more opportunities you can give them to be responsible as a group for their work, the better their communication skills will become.

Analysing talk

Planning and learning necessarily involve talk, and it can be very helpful for children to see how valuable such talk is, and how it can

best be organised to contribute to a successful outcome.

The activities in this section suggest structures for organising the oral sharing of information and ideas. They allow groups to pursue related investigations in parallel, so that all the class can share in the findings of each group.

Activity 10 asks children actively to analyse the talk taking place in a group. Such introspection can be a valuable way of learning the means, values and limitations of discourse.

7. Envoying

Age range
Five to eleven (younger children will need help).

Group size
Small groups.

What you need
No special requirements.

What to do
This activity can take place as part of any other activity that involves groups of children discussing or planning something. For example, the

class may be divided into five groups, each with the task of evaluating a device in a design and technology context before they move on to generate designs.

Stop the discussion in all the groups and send the children from one group as envoys to each of the other groups. These envoys should:
• tell the other groups what has been discussed in their group;
• find out what the other groups have considered;
• report what they have found out to their own group.

It is possible to repeat this process by having other groups sending out envoys, so that all the groups have a chance to hear what the other groups have discussed. Each group is then able to consider, and perhaps modify, their original ideas.

NB: Envoying inevitably begins as an artificial device for the sharing of group knowledge. It is probably best to acknowledge this with the class when you first introduce it. However, after using it a few times, the process will become considerably more natural.

8. Jigsaws

Age range
Seven to eleven (this activity can be adapted for younger children).

Group size
Small groups.

What you need
No special requirements.

What to do
This activity is a way of pooling ideas, and should be done in conjunction with another activity, for example, information-gathering on a visit or from books. The children should carry out their initial information-gathering in small groups of four or five.

Once they have shared their ideas in small groups, reassign everyone to new groups by numbering the members of each group from one to four or five. Collect together all the 'ones', all the 'twos' and so on. Tell these new groups that they are 'expert' groups, and assign them each to a different specific aspect of the topic. They can draw on all the different information that has been collected across the class.

Finally, disband the expert groups and ask the children to reassemble in their original groups. They can now share the work of all the expert groups and use this to carry out further tasks.

NB: As with envoying, this can initially appear rather contrived, but when the system has been used a couple of times, the children will be able to see the advantages of being able to specialise in their investigations, but also being able to access everyone else's specialised knowledge.

9. Rainbows

Age range
Seven to eleven (this activity can also be adapted for younger children).

Group size
Small groups.

What you need
No special requirements.

What to do
This is a different way to organise a final report-back session on a project, instead of having the original working groups reporting back to the whole class.

At the final session give each member of each working group a colour (red, orange, yellow and so on). Collect together all the children with the same colour and ask each new group to share with each other the information they gathered in their original groups, and to prepare a final report which draws on all their work.

10. Goldfish bowl

Age range
Nine to eleven.

Group size
Any size.

What you need
No special requirements.

What to do
This activity is designed to help children analyse their own talk, as an occasional way of helping them to focus on the practices that they are employing in group discussion.

The technique can be used with groups of children who are more confident with discussion and who are interested in the processes of how they work together.

At some point during a group activity, ask one child to stop participating and instead become an observer. Ask her to note what is being said as the group continues its work. Who speaks? Who interrupts? How? Who listens – and who does not listen? Does anyone dominate the discussion? Is anyone silent? Are there breakthroughs in agreement? How are conflicts or disagreements resolved?

Once the child has observed the group for about ten minutes, ask her to rejoin the group and share her

observations with them. Do the rest of the group agree with the observer's analysis?

Kinds of talk

This final group of activities is concerned with different kinds of talking and listening. It consists of games and exercises that encourage attention to words and their place in communication. The activities develop talking and listening skills in a direct way, but should be seen as exercises that help development, rather than as end-products in their own right.

11. Rhymes and rhythms

Age range
Five to eleven.

Group size
Any size, although a small group of six to eight including yourself may be best at first.

What you need
A dictionary.

What to do
Sit with the children in a circle and take turns to produce words that rhyme. This calls for careful listening skills in deciding which words are appropriate. You may want to use a dictionary to check that words offered are 'real', and you might allow the group to vote on whether they think a word offered rhymes or not. If the children are unable to

think of an appropriate word then they or the teacher can provide a word to start off a new rhyming chain. Older children could also write down the words that the group produce.

Suitable words to start off with depend on the age and experience of the children in the group. Use simple short words like 'log', 'sad' or 'flat' with younger children and words with more complex sounds such as 'piano', 'drum' and 'percussion' with older children. You might be interested to know that the word 'orange' is one of the very few words in English that is supposed to have no true rhymes!

Alternatively, ask pairs or small groups of children to string rhyming words together into phrases – these may be nonsensical, but ought to sound good! See which group can produce the longest string of words and then share them with the rest of the class.

Try similar activities matching the rhythms of words in a short phrase or sentence.

Further activity

These activities may well lead to spoken poetry or verse (which can be much more effective for children than asking them to write poetry).

12. Onomatopoeia and alliteration

Age range

Five to eleven.

Group size

Any size: a small group of six to eight including yourself may be best at first.

What you need

No special requirements.

What to do

Onomatopoeic words are words that sound like the noise they describe – plop, sniff and burp are three examples. Ask the children to think of as many different onomatopoeic words as they can. This will involve, of course, saying the words to each other and listening carefully to judge if they do indeed sound like the noise.

Alliteration is where a series of words in a sentence begin with the same letter or, more precisely, the same sound. Again, to check that words have the same sound, it helps if the children say the sentence out loud for someone else to listen and check.

Which group can produce the longest meaningful alliteration? (It is permissible to include one or two short linking words that don't start with the appropriate sound.)

13. Speaking without words!

Age range

Seven to eleven.

Group size

Groups of three or four, coming together to form a larger group, perhaps the whole class.

What you need

Paper, pencils, card.

What to do

Write some simple messages on the cards, for example: 'I'm hungry', 'What's the time?', 'I've lost my book', and so on. Let each child in each group take a card and take turns to try to communicate to the other members of the group what the message says without speaking or writing. To avoid them miming syllables and words, ask the children to imagine that they don't share the same language. This will make them concentrate on the meanings of the messages.

Add some more difficult messages, for example: 'Could I borrow your pencil?', 'How long is it to lunch-time/the end of the day?' or 'My mum says that I must go straight home tonight'. Finally, try some

really difficult phrases, such as 'I've got a pet guinea pig', 'There are chips for lunch today', or 'Would anyone like to play rounders?'

Ask the children to keep a note of particular difficulties they have. Then call the groups together to discuss the ways that they have found for communicating without words. What sort of messages presented the most difficulty? What strategies did they devise to solve the problems? What did the difficult messages have in common, that made for problems?

Further activities
This work leads the children towards analysing everyday language. It encourages them to look at the kinds of speech that can be translated into easily understood gestures, and the words and phrases that give difficulty. Do verbs or nouns present more problems? What kinds of nouns are easiest? Can the children devise easy messages and difficult messages of their own? Can they evolve a sign language that copes with all eventualities?

14. Alphabet sentences

Age range
Seven to eleven.

Group size
Five or more children.

What you need
The alphabet written out (without 'x' and 'z').

What to do
Ask the children to sit in a circle. Let one child start by saying a word – any word. The next child must then think of a word beginning with either the next or previous letter of the alphabet (missing out 'x' and 'z'). It has to be a word that can be added to the first word to make part of a sentence. The third child should add another word and so on. As each word is added to the beginning or end of the string the child should repeat the whole string

raining so torrentially, umbrella's very wet.....?

verbal communication is effective? Would it be better with words? Could a person, if she chose to, *not* communicate in this non-verbal way?

of words as the sentence is formed. For example:
man → little man → little man nodded → little man nodded off → knobbly little man nodded off... and so on.

15. Non-verbal communication

Age range
Seven to eleven.

Group size
Pairs, groups of three or the whole class.

What you need
Paper, pencils.

What to do
People communicate through their facial expressions and the way they hold their body, as well as through words. It can be interesting for children to find out how effectively they can 'listen' to communications that are not spoken.

Brief two or three children to observe other children as they work, noting down what they think the child they are observing is feeling or thinking about from his posture and expression.

Alternatively, you could ask the whole class to observe you doing something – perhaps you could come into the classroom in a hurry, find that someone has rearranged some of the classroom equipment, get rather annoyed at this, look around for who could have done it, give up and put the equipment straight and then find a piece of a child's work that is really rather good and pleases you, and so on. When you've completed your 'act', talk through it with the class: what did they observe and what did they deduce?

Further activity
Have a class discussion about how people communicate. Do the children think that non-

16. Words without meaning?

Age range
Seven to eleven.

Group size
Any size.

What you need
Paper, pencils.

What to do
Just as we can communicate without words, some words we use mean nothing or at most, very little; for example, 'um', 'er', 'I mean to say', 'well', and so on.

Ask the children to collect as many examples of such words and phrases as they can. Why do they think people use them? Do these sorts of words change? Could they listen to one another talking about something and keep a record of how often they let these sorts of word slip into what they are saying?

CHAPTER 2

Reporters

A reporter does more than simply transmit a message: she selects the information, sifts through it, evaluates it, and transforms it into a story. This chapter looks at how children develop the critical faculties that enable them to listen creatively and selectively, to process and develop ideas, and to talk about them in an interesting manner to a selected audience.

There is no such thing as an objective report. In any report it is always someone's viewpoint that is being expressed or someone's values that determine the selection of 'facts'. What the reporter thinks to be important or relevant will depend both on her own conceptions of these qualities and on her interpretation of what the audience thinks to be important, interesting and newsworthy.

Some of the activities included in this chapter are games or devices that are designed to offer a way into the development of a specific skill. They are intended to be used only as temporary ploys, to be dropped and forgotten when the children have moved on. They require the teacher to listen to and analyse the children's reports. This should be followed by an analysis of their performance, the identification of stumbling blocks and the selection of appropriate activities that may help the children overcome them and develop further.

Other activities are more substantive, providing ideas that can be returned to again and again as the curriculum context demands. These activities involve children synthesising a variety of spoken language and listening skills with a high degree of complexity.

Aspects of reporting

Telling someone about something that happened sounds an easy thing to do. However, as anyone who has been involved in describing an accident or incident will know, it is a considerably more complex affair than it might at first appear. Simply retelling what happened involves making a complicated series of judgements:
• What does the person I am telling this to already know about the context, and what additional information must I give?
• Which points do I need to include in my report?
• In which order should I present the points if I am to keep the listener's interest and be clear and understandable?

Audience

Children sometimes need to be reminded who their audience is when they are reporting something. If the person they are talking to is well known to them or has shared aspects of the experience with them, then they can (and will) make a great many assumptions about

the listener's knowledge of the context. Much of a child's early speech is to an audience of family and close friends. They naturally make inferences about what is being told to them. Very often, the child will use gestures to make points quickly and unambiguously, for example, pointing to 'that tree there' is a concise way of conveying the tree's location to an audience that can see it.

In a primary classroom the audience will again share many experiences with the speaker. They probably live in the same streets, play together, go on outings from school together and so on. Therefore, an event can be reported with a number of omissions, leaving out anything that is a matter of common knowledge. However, very young children will often

make the assumption that everyone has a similar set of understandings and perceptions to their own. Soon, they will begin to realise that other people don't always know what they themselves know, and that they may need additional information. The work of Margaret Donaldson (*Children's Minds* [1978] Fontana) shows that infant-aged children are often able to identify the perspective of another person. But they may still need to stop and consider, albeit briefly, to whom they are talking, and review what that audience will and will not already know.

To help facilitate this skill, it is useful to try to arrange for the children in a class to speak with as wide a range of audiences as they can: not just with their classroom and playground peers and the teacher, but also with other children, visiting adults and so on.

Accuracy

Most reports are intended to be accurate. Reporters want to tell it 'as it is', which means that they will need to develop skills of investigation. A reporter selects items of information, honing down the details to encapsulate the essential elements of the story. Of course, each person's definition of the essential will be different, so the selection may vary. There is no such thing as a wholly objective report: the preconceptions of the reporter will filter 'the facts', and in any case the reporter will only have access to a limited number of facts before compiling his account.

Accuracy is still an important goal and as reporters children need to be encouraged to strive towards it. Equally, children who receive reports need to be able to recognise that what they are told will inevitably reflect the unconscious biases of the reporter and may also be the result of a conscious

selectivity. Several of the activities in this chapter are designed to help children explore why and how reports need to be evaluated.

Setting the scene

A reporter often needs to do more than recount the facts. She will need to include descriptions and details that contextualise and help the audience identify with aspects of the story. Pulling out the important elements that do this will be consciously a more subjective process than

selecting the factual details of the story. For example, one reporter may include a brief description of the location and of the demeanour of one of the main characters; while another reporter of the same event might mention the unusual weather and describe the appearance of the same character. Both are correct and accurate, and no audience wants to have *all* the details. So the reporter must decide which details he thinks best convey the atmosphere of the story, and how best to include them.

Children need to be helped with this selection. They need to be shown how to impose a discipline of selectivity, to include the bare bones of the story, and at the same time to

see that a bald narrative may not be enough. Asking the key questions – who, what, where, when and how – may help with selectivity, but may also lead to an over-structured and formal style of reporting. Therefore, rather than suggesting such a formula to children, at least in the early stages, it is better to use the 'who, what, where, when and how' questions yourself as a mental check-list when you evaluate a child's report. This will enable you to give help in the form of identifying an omission, for example, 'You haven't told me where this happened'.

A sense of sequence

While it may seem most logical to report on a happening by starting at the beginning, moving on to what came next, carrying on till you reach the end and then stopping, this rarely makes for an interesting

report. Of course, the sequence of events is very often vital in a report, and reports are often difficult to follow if events and ideas are not covered in a logical order. However, it can make for a more interesting account if the reporter includes, early on in her account, the basic facts and details that keep the listener wanting to hear more.

This way of reporting is not always easy to teach. Children have to be shown how to break up the sequence in a way that works and still maintain the sequence so that at the end of the report the listener has a clear understanding of what happened and when. (Similar skills are explored in Chapter 4.)

Spontaneity

Reporters often write up their reports, but the activities in this chapter are concerned only with oral reports. This calls for a spontaneity and speed of response that may not be so necessary when accounts are written down.

Many of the activities in this section could be used as helpful initial activities to be done before writing. However, there is a danger that oral reporting is seen simply as an introduction to writing. This will encourage some children to devalue oral reporting, so that they take part in it reluctantly, feeling that the more that they say, the greater the quantity of writing they will be expected to do.

Activities for the class

The activities in this chapter are divided into sections, but they are not meant to be tackled in a particular sequence. It is important that you select the activities according to the needs of your class or of particular children in your class. Listen to their reports and analyse what needs to be improved. Are the children jumbled in their presentations? Do they omit important background information or scene-setting points? Do they consider their audience's needs? When you have established what problems they have, select activities that will help them.

Reporting skills

The activities in this section are intended to help the children to analyse the elements of a report and to recognise some of the things that need to be included.

1. So what happened?

Age range
Five to eleven.

Group size
Individuals or small groups.

What you need
No special requirements.

What to do
After an educational visit, rather than ask the class to write about it, nominate some children to present an oral report on the visit to the rest of the class. This could be done prior to a report in an assembly. Ask them to describe what they learned from the occasion. They may need encouragement to move away from a purely factual description and to link their report to their evaluation.

Either record the report or make notes, so that you can help the children (either in a small group or as a class) to think about how the report might be improved.
• Were the events covered in a sensible order? At an early stage, this probably means in chronological sequence.
• Did the report relay the basic information about the trip – where the children went to, who went and when?
• Was there a sense of excitement?
• Were the wrong kinds of information included? (Do we really want to know what was in the sandwiches or who went to the lavatory?)

Help the children to establish a guide for what to include in an oral report.

Further activities
Maintain the practice of asking some children to report orally on out-of-school visits.

Encourage these reporters to develop and refine their skills, and use the oral reports as a preliminary stage to writing (but don't do this so frequently that it becomes inhibiting). Move on to Activity 2 below.

2. Report preparation

Age range
Seven to eleven. (This activity can be adapted for younger children.)

Group size
The whole class, divided into small groups.

What you need
No special requirements.

What to do
Before making an educational visit, discuss with the children the kind of oral report that they might prepare, as a group or class, for the rest of the school or for another class. What sort of things will the other children want to know? Can any initial preparation be done before the visit, such as asking particular children or groups to investigate particular aspects of the trip?

After the visit has been completed, ask individual children or groups to present their initial reports to each other. Discuss with the class how these could be sequenced to give an interesting account of the visit and how each part might be improved – by including more detail or taking out repetitions, by concentrating on particular incidents or by setting the scene more fully.

Remember, however, that the objective is an *oral* report, so try to resist the temptation to write things down or to make notes. Ask the children to rely on their memory. As they work on their oral accounts, the narratives will begin to vary, they will embellish and omit certain aspects. Help them identify the changes that they make and discuss with them whether or not these are improvements and how best to include the changes that they want.

Finally, the children can present the finished form to their audience.

Further activity

Discuss with the children the idea of making preparations to give a report. Try to develop with them the skills that a television or radio news-reporter has of carefully observing or investigating something and then reporting on it concisely, but with all the relevant information.

3. Sounds good – or does it?

Age range
Seven to eleven.

Group size
Groups of six or eight.

What you need
No special requirements.

What to do
This activity is a variation of an old game. Divide each group in half and tell both sides that they are going to report on the same incident or activity. This must be something that all the children have experienced. However, one side will present all the positive aspects, and the other will make negative comments.

For example, one side may begin, 'We went on a school trip yesterday', to be countered with, 'And it rained all day'.

The dialogue might continue:
• 'But nobody got wet, because we went by coach, and the trip was to the museum.'
• 'It was a very long visit, and we didn't get back till late.'
• 'But that was because it was so interesting being there: we really liked the dinosaur bones that were millions of years old.'
• 'Except for the bit where we had to write about it.'
• 'But we did have more time drawing pictures than writing....'

This activity encourages the children to think quickly, listen carefully to the opposition and develop the idea that there can be two sides to every story.

Further activity
Ask the children to report on sports matches, another class's assembly, project work, local events and so on.

Sense reports

Descriptive powers are analysed in the activities in this section. They explore the senses, developing vocabulary and structures that will help children to set the scene in their reports.

4. Describe a smell

Age range
Five to eleven.

Group size
Groups of up to six.

What you need
Half-a-dozen opaque containers with muslin or thin cloth covers, some objects with a distinctive smell, for example: a vanilla pod, a little methylated spirit on cotton wool (take care with this), sandalwood soap, detergent powder, plain yoghurt, a cinnamon stick, beeswax polish, peppercorns, fresh sawdust, mint leaves.

What to do
Place one of the smelly objects in each container and cover them with muslin or a thin cloth. Ask the children to take it in turns to select a container and sniff at the contents. They should not try to identify the contents of each container – though this might be an interesting way to end the session – but should report on what the smell reminds them of. For example, a cinnamon stick might remind them of spicy biscuits, or of fresh baking, or a snack on holiday.

After the first child has told the rest of the group what his impressions were, the container should be passed to the next child, who should then add her own perceptions.

In this way, spoken word-pictures of a particular odour develop, built up between the group. Once one container has been passed around, move on to the next.

Further activity
Each group might choose one child to act as scribe, jotting down what the children say. A poem or another piece of collaborative writing might emerge from this work, if you wanted to extend the work in this direction. Marcel Proust wrote a series of novels, *A La Recherche du Temps Perdu*, all based on recollections from the odour of 'petites madeleines'!

5. Talking about touch

Age range
Five to eleven.

Group size
Groups of three to six.

What you need
A cardboard box, a collection of items that feel different, for example, bits of hard and soft plastic (a LEGO brick, a sweet wrapper, an old credit card, a plastic beaker, a bottle top); a large nut and a bolt, a screw, pieces of cloth (velvet, silk, nylon), a nail-brush, a washing-up glove, a nail, a feather, a twig, some straw or dried grass... you could even risk including some toy slime!

What to do
As with the previous activity, the purpose of this activity is for the children to describe to

the other members of the group what the various objects feel like, rather than to identify them. This is quite difficult to do, especially if the children can see the objects: this is why using a 'feely box' is advantageous. Cut a small hand-sized hole in the side of the cardboard box. You could also add a cloth sleeve to the hole, so that it is impossible for the children to peep inside. Encourage the group to exchange impressions, so that they build up a pattern of words that convey a real sensation of feeling. Help the children to identify and use words that describe sensations of feeling and texture.

Further activities
This activity may lead on to writing. Also, when older children have finished this activity, try a variation using different powders in

envelopes, for example, granulated sugar, icing sugar, custard powder, detergent powder, caster sugar and flour. The children will probably find that describing the feeling of different textured powders is quite difficult.

6. Listening time

Age range
Five to eleven.

Group size
Any size: it may be most convenient with the whole class.

What you need
A tape recording of different sounds, for example, a door-bell, a lavatory flush, a door closing, lighting a match, running a tap, closing curtains, emptying the bath, a bus, a car, footsteps, a police siren, an ice-cream van, or music played by different

instruments (try to include a snatch of Mozart's *Adagio for a Glass Harmonica Solo* (K617a) if you really want to fox them!).

What to do
Play one of the noises or extracts to the children. Ask one of them to report to the others on what the sound was like. Again, try to emphasise description rather than simple identification. Continue by asking other children to add to the report on the noise. Then move on to the next sound.

Alternatively, play the noise to one child so that the rest of the class can't hear it (using a headset might be one way to arrange this). Can the child then describe the sound well enough for the rest of the class to be able to identify it?

Further activity
Children could make their own collections of sounds to listen to.

7. The subject is the object

Age range
Five to eleven.

Group size
The whole class.

What you need
A revival of the old-fashioned 'object table'.

What to do

Bring in a few interesting objects, and encourage the children to contribute some of their own. Ask one child to select an object that she did not bring in herself, and to tell the rest of the children a story about what she thinks was the history of the object.

Telling the tale

The activities in this section look at a variety of contexts in which reports are given and encourage the development of the ability to select appropriate styles of reporting.

8. Radio commentator

Age range
Five to eleven.

Group size
Two or three children per available tape recorder.

What you need
One or more reasonably good-quality tape recorders, ideally with a separate microphone.

What to do
This activity works best when going on a class visit to an exhibition, a countryside site or a display of some sort. It is particularly suitable for children who have difficulty writing.

Ask a group of children to pretend that they are producers of a radio programme. They can then use the tape recorder to give a commentary on where they are going and what they see on the trip. They can also record short interviews with people that they meet and record background noises, such as bird song and music.

Back in the classroom, with the help of a double cassette recorder, a group of children should be able to edit the original tape by re-recording fragments on to a new tape. They could be asked to produce a fifteen minute programme in this way.

Further activities
Use this method to keep records of some scientific activities or of a day in the life of the school.

With older children, different groups could take on more ambitious projects and exchange tapes between classes.

9. Weather report

Age range
Five to eleven, with appropriate variations.

Group size
Groups of up to six.

What you need
Large sheets of paper, coloured pens, a tape recorder, Blu-Tack.

What to do

Ask the groups of children to prepare and present a television weather report. Older children might like to take on the idea of adding a forecast. Make maps and use Blu-Tack to stick on the weather symbols. You could also tape the musical jingle that some television channels use to introduce their weather reports.

The children's report can be straightforward and factual, for example, on the previous day's weather. As an alternative, the children could make up a report about some freak weather conditions – storms, snow drifts, flooding and the like – and include mock interviews with people who have been affected.

Further activity

A project on weather recording might follow from this.

10. News report

Age range

Five to eleven, with appropriate variations.

Group size

Small groups.

What you need

No special requirements, but a cardboard television screen might be useful, as might paper picture backdrops, dummy microphones and a tape recording of a television news signature tune.

What to do

Ask the children, either as groups or as a class, to prepare and present their version of an evening news programme. This would be a suitable activity to follow on from Activities 8 to 11 below.

Encourage the children to study how the news programmes are put together, for example, the way that the sports results come at the end and so on.

The children could make up their own news stories or report on what has happened in school. Encourage them to take on different roles – newsreader, on-the-spot reporters, correspondents providing analysis, witnesses, experts and so on.

11. Match report

Age range

Seven to eleven.

Group size

Groups of up to six.

What you need

A tape recorder for each group, a video-recording of a television sports match and report (optional).

What to do

After a games or sports lesson, ask a group of children to prepare a sports report on the event. They could either do this for other members of the group or prepare a television-style presentation. It might help them to get the style right if they were able to study some real television sports reports.

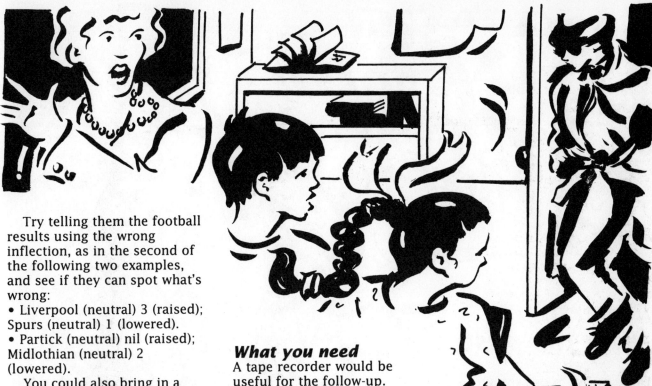

Try telling them the football results using the wrong inflection, as in the second of the following two examples, and see if they can spot what's wrong:
• Liverpool (neutral) 3 (raised); Spurs (neutral) 1 (lowered).
• Partick (neutral) nil (raised); Midlothian (neutral) 2 (lowered).

You could also bring in a video-recording of a sports event and play it with the sound turned off, inviting the children to add their own commentary. This works better if you use athletic events that are relatively short, rather than football matches.

Further activity
Ask different groups of children to record a commentary on a tape recorder and compare their recordings, or try to match the sound tracks to the video-recording. How could improvements be made?

12. Accident report

Age range
Seven to eleven.

Group size
Small groups or the whole class.

What you need
A tape recorder would be useful for the follow-up.

What to do
Without giving your class any warning, stage an 'incident' in the classroom. This could be anything from a visit from a 'stranger' with an urgent and secret message (with a suitably furtive air), to two children from another class coming into the classroom apparently having a furious argument. Deal with the incident and then ask members of the class to say what they saw happen. The children could either then report to members of a group (and perhaps emerge with a consensus account that they present to the whole class), or individuals could report directly to the whole class.

There is often a surprising divergence of views about what happened. Descriptions of what people looked like, and of what was said, can vary wildly. Ask the class to explain why they think their versions differ so much. Which do they think is the most accurate version? You might call back the actors who helped you stage the incident, confronting the class with what they really look like, and ask for their account of what they said.

Ask older children to think about the implications of what they have found in relation to criminal investigations. How accurate are reports by witnesses to a crime likely to be?

Further activities
Groups of children could make a tape-recorded radio news broadcast reporting on the incident, incorporating a news-reader, on-the-spot reporter and interviews with various witnesses, including yourself.

You may want to follow up by working on Activities 16 and 17 on pages 48 and 49.

Reporting from the past

The activities in this section provide some examples of imaginative reporting that help children synthesise historical and oral skills. These ideas and the structures behind the three activities can be extended and varied to match any historical study that your class may undertake.

13. When dinosaurs roamed the earth

Age range
Nine to eleven (perhaps in conjunction with some younger children).

Group size
Groups of six.

What you need
Reference books and materials to support a project on prehistoric life, a tape recorder.

What to do
This activity would fit in well with a class project on prehistoric life, since the children involved will need to have some information on the subject before they begin this activity, although the activity might also be a stimulus to further investigations.

Ask the children to imagine that they are radio reporters transported into the past by a time machine. They have gone back hundreds of millions of years into the past, long before humans existed and when the major form of animal life was the dinosaur. What do they see? What happens?

Ask the children to prepare a 'live' radio broadcast of this. Groups could work collaboratively – they will probably need to do some research – and could add suitable sound effects.

Further activity
Make tape recordings of the finished broadcasts and let other classes borrow and comment on them.

14. In the Blitz

Age range
Nine to eleven (perhaps in conjunction with some younger children).

Group size
Groups of six.

What you need
Reference books and materials for a project on the 1940s, a tape recorder.

What to do

This activity would fit in well with a class project on the Second World War or life in the 1940s.

Collect information about life on the 'home front' during the Second World War. This might involve interviewing older people about their memories (see Activity 15, page 118).

Once the children have researched the background information ask them to prepare a radio account of an air-raid: they could imagine themselves as commentators on the roof-tops or report on what it was like out in the streets or in the shelters during a raid. Different groups could have different locations. Sound effects – not too loud – would add to the verisimilitude!

Further activity

Make tape recordings of the finished broadcasts and let other classes borrow and comment on them.

15. Alongside Guy Fawkes

Age range

Nine to eleven (perhaps in conjunction with some younger children).

Group size

Groups of six.

What you need

Reference books and materials for a project on Guy Fawkes and his time.

What to do

This activity would fit in well with class projects on the Stuarts, Guy Fawkes or Parliament.

Ask the children to imagine that Guy Fawkes invited a reporter to accompany him to various meetings that he had with his co-conspirators, and to the cellars under the House of Commons.... Can they prepare the radio reports of this? They should include a commentator's introduction to the recordings of the conspiracy and a final live account from the cellars at the moment that the guards arrive.

Further activity

Make tape recordings of the finished broadcast and let other classes borrow and comment on them.

Telling the truth

The notions of objectivity and subjectivity, and the fact that some reports may be deliberately untruthful, are explored in these last two activities. They are intended to help children develop the skills of listening carefully and analysing what has been said.

16. Conflicting reports

Age range
Five to eleven.

Group size
Pairs.

What you need
No special requirements.

What to do
Ask two children to report on the same activity, but from different points of view. For example, supporters of different football teams might give very different accounts of the same match, varying from 'It was a walk-over' to 'We was robbed!' Was the foul an accident or was it deliberate?

Other activities which could be reported on might include playground squabbles, disputes over who said what and so on.

Ask the children why different people can see the same event in different ways. It might be worth making the point that there is no such thing as a truly neutral report as we all have preconceptions that colour what we see.

Further activity
Ask the children to find other examples of different people giving different versions of the same thing. Older children might find many examples by studying the news: broadcast news reports are generally better than newspapers at presenting the different sides of a story, often in the person's own words.

17. False report

Age range
Nine to eleven.

Group size
Small groups at first, then the whole class.

I was only taking back what belonged to me, your honour!

What you need
No special requirements.

What to do
In a court of law, witnesses are on oath to report 'the truth, the whole truth and nothing but the truth'. However, this does not always happen: not only do witnesses have different perceptions of the truth (see Activity 16, page 48), but some witnesses may deliberately mislead the court.

Organise a group of four or five children to stage an incident in which a 'crime' is committed. Ensure that the witnesses to the crime only get a partial view of what happens and help the 'guilty' parties to prepare a convincing but totally false alternative story. Then organise the rest of the

class to investigate what has happened and to hold a trial. One group of children could act as the police, another as the prosecuting team and another as the defending team of lawyers. Tell them to collect and prepare evidence, to decide which witnesses to call and what lines of argument to follow. The rest of the children can have roles as jurors.

It is probably best to cast yourself as the judge, as this allows you to control proceedings in role: you can decide what evidence is

permissible, and can 'direct' the lawyers. (It is also fun to insist that the class rise when you enter the room!)

Further activity
Debrief the class after the jury have decided on a verdict and direct their attention back to look at how people report on what has happened.

CHAPTER 3

Instructors

Teachers are quite naturally used to giving instructions, but it can be helpful to step back and consider the complexity of what you are doing when you tell the children what to do.

• You have decided upon and understood what you want to achieve.

• You have separated out the various parts of the process that have to be done.

• You have decided upon the order in which the children should do each part.

• You have decided upon materials and equipment are needed.

• You have reminded children where materials are kept, or introduced them to new equipment or techniques.

• You may have split the tasks into various components and selected specific children for particular aspects.

• You may have demonstrated in some form what you want the groups or the class to do.

• You have presented the instructions using the appropriate vocabulary, explaining new terms and ensuring that the points are understood.

The fact that any teacher does this, or something very similar, fifty times a day doesn't make the task any simpler. Giving someone an instruction is not a simple matter and children will need time and practice to develop the skills needed to become competent givers of instructions.

Analysing the processes involved in making up a set of instructions allows us to identify the skills needed, and watching children struggle to achieve competency in these skills helps us to select strategies and devices that concentrate on those particular aspects that need help. Many of the tasks in this chapter are games that develop the skills of clarity, precision and analysis in an instruction-giving context. In this respect they are a means to an end, rather than activities in their own right.

Children are quite used to creating, finding out and applying rules and instructions to events and behaviour in their lives. The issuing of rules and commands that tell them what to do is an important way for them to see some sort of order and stability in the world. Indeed, one of the ways in which young children learn is through inventing and enforcing rules that explain how things should be. For example, in the field of spoken language, many young children establish that there is a rule for creating the past tense of a verb, namely adding the suffix '-ed' to the present tense form of the verb. This is fine, until they say, 'I seed you'. Though the rule doesn't work in this case, children often go on applying it with remorseless logic, thinking that it *ought* to be the correct word.

Children expect their world – at school, home and play – to be governed by rules and instructions. Most children become quite good at understanding what instructions mean and even at reinterpreting them so that they can be evaded. But they often find it harder to *give* instructions. This chapter is designed so that teachers can choose the activities that enable them to observe and analyse the problems that children encounter in giving instructions and to select and use suitable activities to help the children overcome these problems.

Aspects of instruction-giving

Recognising the problem

Perhaps the first thing to establish is that there is a need for instructions in a particular context. This may be very obvious, for example, when making a cake or playing a game, but there are also instructions to give in less formalised contexts. For example, in tidying up the classroom, or in reading a map, there are procedures to follow that need to be clearly explained. Any form of technological activity (using technology in the broad sense given to it in the National Curriculum – establish a need, plan, design, make and evaluate) will require clear instructions if it is to be passed on from one child to another.

Technology might provide a very useful context for developing children's powers of formulating and giving oral instructions. On many occasions it is possible to ask children, at the conclusion of a successful design, to tell other children what they did. Giving them this sort of exercise will help them to clarify their own thought processes and to recognise the need for instructions in context.

Analysis

Once a need has been recognised, the process to be explained needs to be dissected to establish the important elements. Do all the elements need to be explained? Must some parts be explained first? What aspects are the most complex? Do these need to have separate instructions?

In giving instructions, it is important to be aware of the intended audience. A cookery book aimed at experienced cooks will blithely instruct the reader to make choux pastry or knock up a glaze, while one for complete beginners will start by labelling the parts of the tin-opener! What does one know of the competencies of those receiving the instructions? What forms of shorthand or jargon can be used to simplify the process? Instructions for washing clothes, for examples, have now been refined and processed so that a complex set of rules about water temperature, wringing, drying and ironing can be given in a simple row of icons (see figure below).

Clarity of expression

Describing physical processes can be extraordinarily difficult, especially when relying purely on words. Giving precise instructions on, for example, tying a shoe-lace, is very hard. (The sort of 'instructions' provided for this are usually forms of mnemonics that help ritualise a process that is actually taught by repeated demonstrations.)

It isn't, of course, necessary to put everything into words in everyday instruction-giving, but it can be a useful exercise sometimes to try to do this and to attempt to leave out all the language that goes rather like:

'Well, you stick this thing here up through that bit there, and then down about here through this thingumy'.

Sequence

With really complex instructions, it may be necessary to give them in an order which isn't quite sequential. For example, in a recipe it is quite usual to separate the various components of a meal or a dish and give separate lists of instructions for each. This makes it easier to follow, even though the cook following the instructions has to reformulate the parts into a single pathway of activities.

Sometimes an activity will be too complex to attempt all at once, for the level of ability or experience of the audience. In this case it may be necessary to learn to do the various component elements of a task separately and to practise them in isolation, before bringing them all together in a final set of instructions.

much simpler just to say 'screw the support to the leg'!

Demonstrations

Actually showing another person how something is done is probably the most efficient way of clearly communicating instructions. However, you could put it to the class that there may be occasions when you have to tell someone rather than showing them. For example, while it is often possible to point to a map to explain a route, if you need to call out a car-rescue service by phone, this has to be done verbally.

A great deal of very specific vocabulary is needed when giving instructions. Much of this relates to descriptions of location or movement (and there are important and useful analogies with mathematics too), while others relate to sequences in time. There will also be specific words that express groups of movements or activities and the extent to which these can be used will depend upon the experience of the person being instructed. Imagine the instructions for assembling a piece of furniture if one had to describe exactly how to use a screwdriver – it is

Following instructions

Making up instructions is one part of the process: following them is another. It can be quite salutary – and fun – to try to follow instructions as slavishly as possible, to show how difficult it is to be precise and unambiguous. Several of the activities in this chapter are based on the principle that one child instructs while another child does, and they then compare the results with the intentions. If this approach is adopted, it helps to keep changing the roles of instructor and instructed, so that frustrations do not build up on one side only, and the pair can empathise with each other and recognise the magnitude of the task, rather than the incompetency of their partner!

ACTIVITIES

Getting started

The basic reporting activities in this section should help children appreciate some of the requirements of a good set of instructions.

1. In the dark?

Age range
Five to eleven (younger children will need careful supervision).

Group size
The whole class.

What you need
The school hall, or a similar open space; various obstacles such as tables, chairs, benches and mats; a number of blindfolds.

What to do
Without the children being present, set up the hall with various obstacles. You are creating an unknown country that the children are to explore by touch alone. Bring a group of blindfolded children into the hall and tell them that they have three minutes to begin finding out what the country is like: where are the things in it?

After they have groped their way about, lead them back to the class. They must now try to give instructions to the rest of the class on what they have found, because a second group are going to explore in a similar way. This group will need the first group's information in order to be able to increase their knowledge and help to build the mental picture of the area further. Do the group of instructors find it easy to agree on the information they are passing on, or do they find that they give contradictory accounts?

Let all the children have a go at feeling their way in the unknown country and adding to the group's knowledge.

Ask the class how helpful they found the instructions they had been given by other groups. Were they sufficiently clear for them to build up a mental map of where to go and what to avoid? What sort of instructions would have been better?

Finally, let the children go back into the hall without their

blindfolds to see what they were really up against and to see how much (or how little) it matched their imagination.

Further activity
Repeat the activity, allowing the children to try to make maps for each other. Ask the class to discuss whether this makes the task of giving instructions easier or more difficult, and why.

2. Factory production line

Age range
Seven to eleven (this activity may be adapted for younger children).

Group size
The whole class or large groups.

What you need
Sheets of A4 card (perhaps of different colours), scissors, paper-fasteners, string or thread, colouring pens, photocopiable page 177, adhesive, cotton wool.

What to do
Giving instructions calls for clarity of thought in analysing what is to be done. This activity is designed to help children see how complex a task this can be.

Show a small group of children how to make a dancing clown. First, cut out the template on photocopiable page 177 and use it to trace the shapes on to card. Then cut out the card and colour it

in. Assemble the clown's arms and legs with paper-fasteners and fix the string to the top. You can then complete the clown by decorating it, perhaps with adhesive and cotton wool or glitter. Make sure that the rest of the class are not able to see or hear your explanation. The intention is that the small group of children instruct the rest of the class how to make the clowns. Tell the class that they are now going to produce clowns in a series of production lines. Split the class into loose groups, and assign each of the children who saw you make the clown to a larger group. The one child in each group who knows how to make the clowns will have to give clear instructions to the rest. They will have to divide up the group so that, for example, two cut, three colour, one assembles and so on. They will also have to decide how each task is to be performed, which colours to use, which part to work on, and the order in which things will be done. However, they must not *show* their group what to do, but must instruct them verbally. Arrange the tables in rows so that the groups can sit in a row and perform the tasks they have been told to do.

The children will soon discover that their tasks have not been described to them very clearly and that it is not as easy to do as they had thought. Select another small group of children, one from each group, and show them what to do – again, if at all possible, out of sight of the rest of the class. Then send them back to give instructions together with the first children.

Discuss with the whole class the problems that they have encountered. Some of the 'workers' might like to explain how ambiguous the instructions were; the instructors might point out how difficult it is to explain things clearly. Finally, you will probably need to show the whole class what to do – or dare you rely only on oral instructions?

Further activity
You can easily adapt this idea so that the groups make other things, such as dancing Santas at Christmas time. Discuss with the class the merits and problems of working in production lines. You will find more ideas on this theme in *Bright Ideas: World of Work* (Scholastic Publications, 1989).

3. Which way?

Age range
Seven to eleven (this activity can be adapted for younger children).

Group size
Pairs.

What you need
A screen made from light card (or a cardboard box), paper, pencils.

What to do
Divide a table into two with a cardboard screen so that when two children are sitting opposite each other they cannot see each other.

Ask two children to sit behind the screen and take it in turns to draw a simple diagram, plan or map. The child who is drawing should describe it to her partner, either while she is composing it or when she has completed it. From the spoken description alone, her partner should attempt to draw the same diagram. He is not allowed to ask any questions, he must just listen. When he has finished, the children can compare the results.

Early attempts at this will probably highlight the need to be accurate and precise when giving instructions, especially when describing location, position and direction.

Further activities
• Give the children on both sides of the screen a copy of the same plan or map and ask one to describe a route and the other to trace it on his map.
• Give one child an object to describe and ask the other to draw it from the description given.

4. Follow the route

Age range
Seven to eleven.

Group size
Pairs work best, but this can be easily adapted for small groups of three or four.

What you need
Copies of a street map – perhaps of the local area – for each child.

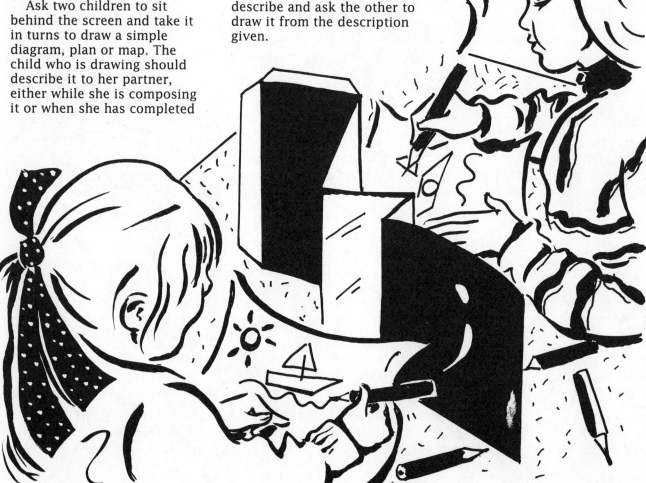

What to do

Give each child a copy of the street map and ask one child in each pair or group to decide upon a route. She should then agree with the other child or children the starting point for this route and ensure that everyone begins at this point on their maps. Then she can give instructions to the other children about where to go to follow the route.

The first time that children try this activity, they will probably give street names, if these are shown on the map. If the map shows the local area, they may also give other information that possibly isn't even on the map, such as 'past the launderette on the corner, then turn left at the sweet shop...'. The other child or children, who shouldn't be able to see the first child tracing the route on her map, must follow her instructions and see if they can finish at the same destination.

Repeat the activity with other children choosing the route and giving instructions.

You could also add various elements to make the task of instruction-giving more complex. For example, you may choose not to allow the child who is following instructions to ask any questions or you may tell the instructor not to use street names, or only to use directions such as left and right or north, south, east and west.

Further activity

Discuss with the class why this activity is so difficult. What techniques can they work out that will help them to give clear instructions? What things are of most help to the followers?

Refining skills

The two activities in this section are designed to help children to refine their precision in giving instructions. They can be used to lead towards more accurate instruction-giving.

5. Building

Age range
Five to eleven.

Group size
Pairs.

What you need
A cardboard screen, a collection of construction materials, such as DUPLO or LEGO, divided into two so that each set has the same items in it.

What to do
Sit the children at a table so that they are either side of the cardboard screen. Ask one of the children to make a model out of her set of construction materials. She must give instructions on what she is doing to the other child, who must follow what he is told. Once the models have been completed the children should compare them and try to work out how the instructions might have been improved.

It may help to limit the number of pieces that the children work with at first, gradually allowing the tasks to become more complex. Ensure that each child takes it in turn to be the instructor and to follow orders. Even with two simple LEGO blocks, there can be 17 different ways of fixing them together, so unambiguous instructions are very difficult to give.

Further activity
Discuss with the class why it is so difficult to give clear instructions. Help them to establish ways of describing the different pieces and of putting them together.

6. Drawing

Age range
Seven to eleven.

Group size
Small groups of four or five.

What you need
Paper, pencils, a blindfold.

What to do
Blindfold one of the children and ask him to imagine a picture – preferably quite a simple one – and describe it to the other children in his group. The other children must try to draw what they are told. When all the drawings are finished ask everyone to compare the results. The child who was blindfolded can say how the pictures match his intentions, or he could draw his own version.

Remember to change the children round so that everyone has a chance to give instructions.

Discuss with the different groups or the whole class the problems that have been met. Did the children who tried later give better instructions? How? Why?

Playing the game

This section uses children's games as a context for giving instructions. These examples suggest teaching strategies which can be adapted to curricular areas that are particularly useful and appropriate for your class.

7. Playground games

Age range
Five to eleven.

Group size
Any size.

What you need
No special requirements.

What to do
Many children's playground games have been passed down, modified and changed over centuries. For example, 'I'm the king of the castle' was played in Roman times. The rules that govern how these games are played have been passed on by word of mouth, but this is not as simple a process as it seems.

Ask a group of children if they can give you a simple set of instructions that explain how a game is played. You should attempt to follow their instructions as literally as possible, to highlight the ambiguities in what they say.

Ask other children to help to see if they can increase the accuracy of the instructions. What sort of words and phrases are needed in order to be clear?

Further activity
Ask the children to make a collection of playground games – perhaps they could make a set of rule books. Ask them to survey the games that are played by children of different ages or across the seasons: how do games change and how are they linked to particular ages?

8. Board game

Age range
Seven to eleven.

Group size
Groups of four to six.

What you need
Card, pens, colouring pens, dice, counters.

What to do
Ask the children to invent a new board game. You could offer some initial guidance or make some restrictions. For example, you may say that the game must help with counting up to a hundred, or help younger children with their maths in some way, or be based on a particular multiplication table.

Once the children have invented the game they must

tell someone else in the class (or the younger children for whom it is intended) the instructions for playing it. Try to insist that they give spoken descriptions of the rules rather than *show* the children what to do.

Can the children follow the instructions? Were they clear enough? Is there a specific order for giving instructions for games that makes things straightforward and not confusing?

Further activities
Children could write down the rules for their games. Are these easier to follow? They might then examine the printed rules of commercially produced board games. Do these have a pattern that the children could follow? Why is this pattern established?

9. A question of sport

Age range
Nine to eleven.

Group size
Small groups.

What you need
No special requirements.

What to do
Ask the group to give you a clear set of rules that explains one or more of the following:

• the off-side rules in football;
• how netball games begin;
• the differences between the rules for singles and doubles at tennis;
• some other similar aspect of a sport with which the children are familiar.

Most children, even if they have a very clear mental picture of how the game operates in practice, find it very difficult to give a simple account of something like this. You will need to help them clarify their points and to present them in a logical sequence.

Alternatively you could ask a group of children to give you a clear set of instructions for making a bed, inflating a bicycle tyre, cooking an omelette, washing a baby or anything that *seems* simple and within the children's everyday experience.

CHAPTER 4

Story-tellers

Stories have been told, so far as we know, from the beginnings of language, and the oral tradition of the story-teller still dominates large sections of the world today. Oral story-telling has a long ancestry and can often prove to be a highly accurate method of transmission, withstanding the changes of time. For example, the story of the Iliad was passed down by word of mouth for over a thousand years before it was first written down: yet the names and events largely accord with the archaeological evidence.

Stories have been listened to for as long as they have been told, and listeners respond by retelling the stories, by modifying and extending them. So many stories for young children lend themselves to sequels – for example, the hero of Eric Carle's The Very Hungry Caterpillar (Picture Puffin) could spend another week eating his way through more kinds of food, or Jill Murphy's bear in Peace at Last (Macmillan) could be kept awake by more noises. In the latter case the children will have already recognised the structure and the repetition, and they need only invent the sound, because they will know that Mr Bear still couldn't sleep... ' "Oh No!", said Mr Bear, "I can't stand THIS." So he went off to sleep in the ...'.

BACKGROUND

Telling a story is both simple and complex. Stories have their own particular narrative forms and their own specific conventions about how they are told, to whom and when. Children pick up and take on the idioms of each kind of story that they encounter, so that the forms and characters become almost ritualised: they know the kind of things to expect when a story begins, 'Once upon a time...', and how the story ought to end. They know the kind of activities that Anansi will get up to, the sorts of characters he will meet and the tricks he will play to outwit them. This predictability helps children create and tell their own stories, using familiar structures as models on which to base their ideas. The simplicity of the predictable form allows the child to safely impose his own complexity upon it, in a way that he is not able to do in written form till the upper stages of the junior school.

Listening to stories

One of the major starting points for the development of children's oracy and literacy is listening to stories. From these experiences come both the desire to read, to unlock the source of the stories and to take control of them, and the desire to imagine their own story, that will grip and entertain the audience in the same way as the original.

Story-telling in the infant classroom needs, therefore, to be frequent, to mix old favourites with new stories and to be the basis for oral explorations into and out from the story. For example, Jill Murphy's story *On the Way Home* (Macmillan) tells the story of Clare, going home from the park with a cut knee. She offers different explanations to the friends she meets on the way to account for the injury – involving giants, ghosts, crocodiles and monsters. Each explanation is presented in a format that both offers security of form and

allows for the fright of finding something equally horrible on the next page. It is the work of seconds to extend the story, allowing children to suggest what Clare will say to her next friend when he asks her 'How did it happen?' and all the class can join in with the familiar repeated phrases.

The Shopping Basket by John Burningham (Armada Lions), offers a similar repetitive structure involving a boy going home from the shop. The boy meets various wild animals that bar his way, but he manages to trick his way past them using the contents of his shopping bag to distract them. If you restocked his basket with a fresh selection, you could let your class tell each other whom he met next, what he gave them and what happened to them.

Even young children can join in. *On Friday Something Funny Happened* by John Prater (Picture Puffin) offers a series of prosaic statements, such as

'On Monday, we went to the shops' which are illustrated by pictures of two children indulging in outrageous behaviour. Read the text and let the children say what happened. Finish the text, close the book and make up more words: the children will furnish the descriptions of pictures that exist only in their imaginations.

Stories like this introduce a sense of the pattern within a book. Stories that come from the same author can do the same: we all know, for example, the sort of things that the little girl in the 'My Naughty Little Sister' books by Dorothy Edwards (Mammoth) will do, even though we can't predict the plot.

Stories that belong to a particular genre extend this pattern. Ask a class of seven-

year-olds about what happens in fairy stories, and you can get them to construct the framework that most tales fall into, the stock characters, the rises and falls of the plot and so on.

When listening to stories children begin to see the scaffolding that supports particular kinds of stories, and can begin to replicate these supports themselves. Encourage them to discuss their own variations with each other, working collaboratively to identify improvements that need to be made, gaps to be filled and excisions to be made.

Older children, towards the top of the junior school, will enjoy listening to more varied and perhaps less predictable stories. Longer novels can become serials, and serial books can lead to an enormous variety of oral work. For example, reading George Orwell's *Animal Farm* (Penguin) to a class of ten-year-olds led to long discussions on how the farm was organised at different stages in the story and how these changes had come about.

Gene Kemp's *The Turbulent Term of Tyke Tiler* (Puffin) was read without much discussion, till we reached the point in the final pages where it is revealed that Tyke, who had indulged in extravagant cheekiness to school staff, spine-chilling adventures out of school and finally climbs on to the school roof to ring the disused bell on the last day of term, is a girl. Total disbelief from at least half the class. They insisted that we scan back through the book to try to find where it was stated that Tyke was a boy (which they couldn't find, because it isn't there – Kemp is very careful with her use of pronouns). Then a furious discussion of whether a girl would do these things and how the author had tricked them.

A sense of audience is important to a story-teller. Gene Kemp certainly judged her typical audiences well with *Tyke Tiler*, and children telling stories also need to think about their audience. Typically, stories are told for consumption inside the class itself, but with a little imagination they can often be extended to other classes, to the whole school and to parents. Ask the children to consider the changes they might need to make as they tell and retell their stories for different audiences. What will the audience know and expect? How much will these expectations be met? How often (and how) will they be broken?

If children tell their stories, rather than write them, they

develop an immediate sense of audience as they see the reactions on the faces in front of them. Writing a story down can sometimes, with some young children, interfere with this particular sense of purpose. The mechanics of writing get in the way of the story. (This is not to argue that children shouldn't write stories – just that sometimes they should be encouraged to tell them orally.)

Children can work together to develop a story. Everyone can contribute ideas, additions and story-lines, and then share the telling in some way. Many of the activities in this chapter which involve puppets, flannel-graphs and overhead projectors are based on the idea of collaborative story-telling.

Stories that children tell, like the stories they write, need to have certain basic characteristics – atmosphere, a sense of place, character development and so on. These can be easier to concentrate on if the children don't simultaneously have to write down their thoughts. Work occasionally with a group of children, helping them to develop the way in which characters are described. Ask questions about the characters, their past, how they look, the way that they do certain things and so on. Talk with them about the way the words sound and how they can be strung together to build up pictures in the head that convey a sense of atmosphere.

Encourage groups or individuals to work on a series of short stories, with characters that can develop from one story to the next. You could then offer the children a series of five-minute slots at story-time for a week.

Story-telling activities

The activities in this chapter focus on children telling their own stories rather than reacting to stories that are read to them.

ACTIVITIES

On their own

The ideas in this section focus on developing stories within particular genres, so that children identify, follow and occasionally flout the conventions of a genre. This will build up children's confidence in telling and listening to stories, and help them discover the rules and parameters.

1. Fairy tale

Age range
Five to nine.

Group size
Any size.

What you need
No special requirements.

What to do
Most children will already be familiar with fairy stories, but you could begin this activity by retelling a few old favourites.

Discuss with the children what fairy stories are about. For example, very few of them actually involve fairies and most involve someone struggling against a hard life! The children may meet various types of character which are rather similar from story to story. Sometimes there are tasks to be achieved, or stronger or more powerful people to overcome, usually by some kind of trick. There is often some powerful person to be cut down to size, before the main character gets his or her fortune, or a beautiful bride or handsome groom: and of course, the story always ends with the hero or heroine living happily ever after. (This genre is very effectively parodied in Robert Musch's The Paper Bag Princess (Scholastic) which

might be a useful way of introducing a discussion of the conventional attributes of the fairytale).

Ask the groups of children if they can make up their own fairy story, remembering some of the things they have found out about how traditional fairy stories are constructed. Ask them to tell their stories to each other, and let the listeners suggest improvements. Finally, the stories could be told to the whole class or acted out.

2. Travellers' tales

Age range
Five to eleven.

Group size
Any size.

What you need
No special requirements.

What to do
Over a period of time, ask different children to tell a story about something that happened to them on holiday or about a place that they have visited. The story need not necessarily be true, although it should be rooted in reality.

It may help to talk individually with each child before he tells his story. For example, you could ask how she is going to begin – with a gripping start or by setting the scene? Does she need to introduce the characters involved in the story at the beginning or to describe the place, or will this come across best if brought out in the course of the story? How will it end?

If a child tells a story to a group of children, perhaps they could work together to refine and improve it before taking it to the next group. In this way the story can be polished and embellished, so that it is barely recognisable.

Favourite stories could be told again, after a decent interval.

Further activity
Work with another teacher so that when stories have been suitably improved, the children can try them out on a fresh audience.

3. It's a dog's life

Age range
Five to eleven.

Group size
Small groups reporting to the whole class.

What you need
Books about animals (for reference purposes).

What to do
Ask a small group of children to prepare themselves to tell the life story of a particular animal. They will need to decide on the type of animal (or you could give this to them), its name and the major stages in its story. Encourage the children to work collaboratively in their groups and to tell the story, rather than read it, adding sound effects if they like.

The children may need to research their animal for ideas and factual information, but urge them to make it an interesting story, rather than just an accurate description of the animal's life cycle.

You could read the children abridged versions of, or

life-stories, such as E.B. White's *Charlotte's Web* (Puffin), or *The Call of the Wild* by Jack London (Hamlyn). You could even be adventurous and try something like *Animal Farm* by George Orwell (Penguin).

Discuss with the children what makes for a 'good' animal story, for example, struggling against the odds, encountering different people or other animals and finally ending up with a more comfortable life. Do the children want their story to conform to this pattern, or to shake it up in some way? If so, how can they most effectively do this?

The children can widen the audience for the story, getting feedback at each stage so that the story develops and improves with the telling.

4. Ghost story

Age range
Seven to eleven.

Group size
Any size.

What you need
No special requirements.

What to do
One of the benefits of introducing a particular type or genre of story is that it becomes possible to discuss particular idioms or styles that make it successful. For example, telling a ghost story, rather than reading it, calls for

a particular way of speaking and unfolding the story. The scene must be set carefully – there should be a great emphasis on descriptions of settings that are ominous or spine-chilling, full of the feeling that something unexpected is about to happen.

Ask the children to work collaboratively in small groups on a ghost story that is to be told (rather than written and read out aloud). Encourage them to break away from an unfolding narrative style, and

not to explain everything: to keep something mysterious back to the end.

As they work on their story, they can practise telling it to each other, and then try it out on another group and ask for suggestions for improving it.

Finally, the story could be told to the whole class.

5. The story of a coin

Age range
Seven to eleven.

Group size
Small groups, leading to the whole class.

What you need
Old and new coins.

What to do
Discuss with the children where a particular coin from your purse or pocket may have been before it turned up in your possession. Choose a fairly old ten pence piece, read out the date and work out with the children how many years it has been passing from person to person. Where has it been since it left the Mint? Through how many hands? What has it been used to buy? Has it ever been lost or stolen?

Ask the groups of children to create their own stories about the coin and tell them out loud as though the coin could speak. Different members of the group could take on different episodes in the story, perhaps each time the coin passes on to its next owner.

This kind of story may develop much faster than some of the other suggestions, because of the general lack of connection between the various episodes.

Two at a time

The activities in this section aim to develop the way children collaborate to tell a story, showing how ideas can be shared together.

6. Phone line

Age range
Five to nine.

Group size
Pairs.

What you need
With younger children, toy phones might be useful accessories.

What to do

The idea of this activity is that one child pretends to tell the other a story over the phone. However, the other child must also try to tell her story. Both children can't talk at the same time, so each has to start when the other one gives him a break. Also, because they can't see each other, the children have to make sure that they describe things, rather than show each other. This can get tricky...!

Further activity

Get two pairs of children to tell their stories at the same time, and give them a crossed line. You will need to control how the 'crossing' takes place: point very clearly at the one child who can be heard on the line and insist that only she speaks.

The resulting stories become unexpected, uncontrollable – and quite interesting to the audience!

7. Stop and carry on

Age range
Seven to eleven.

Group size
Two teams of two to four children.

What you need
No special requirements.

What to do

This is a variation of a popular radio panel-game. Start the activity with one team telling a story, and at a random point ask the other team to continue the story. This makes for good listening skills in itself.

Give the two sides different endings to work towards and ask them also to try not to let their opponents finish first. They will have to couple listening skills with the need to manipulate the story in a very specific direction.

Further activity

There are many extensions and variations to this activity. For example, you could provide each team with specifically worded closing lines which they must reach in order to win.

8. Never-ending story

Age range
Seven to eleven.

Group size
Teams of two to four children.

What you need
No special requirements.

What to do

Ask one team to begin to tell a fantasy story. At a random point, signal to the other group to carry on telling the story. They must do this by moving the location of the story (preferably dramatically), or bringing in a new character. In this way, separate episodes are created.

Try to help them to finish off the episode that they have been put into, and then to establish the outline of their contribution before they too are interrupted. The one rule you could impose is that no team can finish the story.

Further activity

When the story comes back to a team for the second or third time, encourage them to reintroduce some of the characters that were particular to their previous contribution or to move back to that location in some way, but they must do this in a manner that keeps the plot moving forward. This form of narrative, with episodes, characters that are intermittent, and a range of locations, will contribute to the saga-like quality of the story.

In a group

This final group of activities suggests a variety of contexts for a small group to come together to create and tell a story in a performance for other children in the class.

9. Magnetic tale

Age range
Five to nine.

Group size
Two to four children.

What you need
A magnet board, small magnets or magnetic tape, card, scissors, coloured pens or pencils.

What to do
Ask the children to decide on the different characters that will play a part in their stories. Once they have decided, they should draw the different characters on card, colour them in and cut them out. They can then fix magnets or magnetic tape to the reverse of each character, and use the magnet board to rehearse and develop their story-lines.

One advantage, of a sort, that magnetic figures have over puppets is that they can be moved about less easily. This means that the children need to develop character and motivation through the words that they give to the character, rather than through gesture.

10. Flannel-graph

Age range
Five to nine.

Group size
Two to four children.

What you need
A felt-backed board, pieces of different coloured felt, scissors, latex-type adhesive, a ball-point pen.

What to do
Ask the group to make up characters for a story and then create these characters out of felt, sticking on clothes, drawing faces with ball-point pen and so on. It is possible to change a character's clothes fairly easily, by pressing a fresh set (stuck together) over the existing set. It is also possible, with older children, to make the characters face a particular direction and then to reverse them to face the other way (they'll need more clothes!). This can allow more realistic-looking dialogues to take place.

As the children work, ask questions that help them to create the character, and as they talk they will be able to modify and adjust the appearance of their character.

Scenery can also be added, but aim only to give an impression, or large quantities of felt can be used up very quickly!

Once the children have finished making their characters they can use them to tell the story.

Further activities
• Present the finished story to different classes.
• Older children might prepare a special story for younger children, but they will have to do a little market research to find out what the younger children like to listen to.

11. Puppet time

Age range
Five to eleven.

Group size
Groups of three to six.

What you need
Materials for making simple puppets, for example, old socks, felt, plastic foam, material scraps, sticks, old gloves, card, paper, string and so on.

What to do
Show the children how to make puppets – glove puppets or stick puppets can be made fairly easily, for example – and then encourage them to make their own. A small group of children may make two or three each, a larger group only one per person. As they work, encourage the children to think and talk out loud about the character they are creating. Who is it? What's its name? What does it like doing? Where has it been? Does its appearance help answer these questions?

As the characters begin to emerge, encourage the children to talk together about what the characters might get up to if they came together. Who would say what to whom? What would they do? Who would become friends with whom? Which ones would argue? Who would play tricks together? Gradually, as the puppets are being made, a series of story-lines and incidents will develop. All that remains is for the group to agree on a sequence that creates a story, and the play is begun.

Further activities

If the children make up several good story-lines, suggest that they turn them into separate scenes in a longer story, rather than trying to string all of them together in a single scene.

Encourage the group to vary the numbers of puppets in use at any one time; there is often a natural desire to have every puppet in action all the time. Talk about the dramatic advantages given by two puppets plotting together, by soliloquies when secret thoughts can be revealed to the audience and by what can be said when characters enter and leave an existing group on stage.

12. Overhead stories

Age range

Nine to eleven.

Group size

Groups of four to eight.

What you need

An overhead projector and screen, transparent paper, card, coloured pens (water soluble), scissors.

What to do

Using an OHP to tell a story has several advantages over flannel-graphs and magnetic story boards. Characters can easily be flipped over and it is possible to draw the same character on a number of sheets to give the impression of movement. For example, arms can be made to wave by flipping over one sheet that has only the arm drawn on it. (However, it is not very easy to get walking effects!) If you are introducing this kind of effect to the group, try to get them to link particular kinds of effect or gesture to individual characters – they don't want them *all* waving!

It may help to begin the activity by showing the group how the OHP works, but they will not need to use it after that until their story is nearly ready for performance.

Another, much faster, way of using the OHP, is to cut characters out of card, and to stick these silhouettes on to transparencies. Encourage the children to use as much detail as possible in the cutting – quick and hurried outline shapes can be very disappointing.

Further activity

OHP stories, because of the enlargement that is possible, make a very good medium for telling stories to a large group – even to the whole school at an assembly.

CHAPTER 5

Discussions

In a discussion, all the participants have equal responsibility and equal control over what takes place. A discussion is one of the most complex ways of organising spoken language, particularly when the group is larger than about half a dozen. To take part successfully in a discussion calls for the simultaneous use of a range of social skills, empathy and decision-making, as well as listening and speaking skills.

Classroom discussions require children to develop and use all these skills. This is not an easy task, but it's not impossible with children of infant or junior school age. It does, however, take time and practice to develop the abilities needed to take part in discussions.

BACKGROUND

It may take several weeks of careful work to bring a class of children unversed in the skills of discussion to the point where they can interact to some purpose, controlling the give and take of conversation themselves. Many classes of children do not get this far. Teachers, understandably, are concerned that discussions can get out of hand, with loud interruptions, arguments and noise, as well as children not putting forward contributions.

This chapter offers suggestions for developing skills to the point at which children can be given the opportunity to discuss matters on their own, although it must be emphasised that the processes will take time and practice to develop.

Discussions must be about something. This may seem rather obvious – but you will need to link your development of discussion to some other area of your curriculum planning. Discussions can be linked to work in history, geography, technology or cross-curricular themes. Whatever is selected, the topic will need certain characteristics:

• there must be more than one possible viewpoint (and these must be represented in the class);
• the children must be interested in the subject;
• the subject should in some way allow the children to draw upon their own varied experiences, whether directly or indirectly.

Features of discussions

Discussions can occur at any point in the classroom and can be carried out in groups of varying numbers; for example, there may be intense discussions in twos and threes, more formally structured groups interacting and sometimes much larger groups

sharing ideas. Many of these will not directly include the teacher, though you may well be involved initially in setting them up. One of the features of many discussions is that they are self-regulating: it is the participants themselves who fix the subject, determine the order of contributions and create the boundaries of what is permissible to discuss and in what manner.

What shall we talk about?

The ability to take part in a discussion involves a variety of skills, and these need to be fostered and developed. It is sometimes assumed that the classroom discussion is the end-point, that the justification for a discussion is the discussion itself. But real discussions have a different function, related to the subject being considered. The discussion allows participants to:
• give their views and provide information;
• consider the views and information of others;
• come to some conclusion on the issue, forming the basis of further action.

Classroom discussions therefore need to have a real purpose. They must have:
• a subject that is important and interesting to children, one that will allow them to put forward their ideas and experiences;
• an objective, in that there is some need to exchange ideas if progress is to be made. Ideas need to be clarified, or perhaps even agreed, so that other events or work can continue.

These requirements cannot wholly be engineered by the teacher: not all children in a group will, at any one moment, have these needs, so it may happen that some children play a minimal part in a discussion. Clearly, one of the teacher's functions is to help as many children as possible find a role in the discussion, but not at the expense of either taking control of the discussion or of regulating it out of existence because not all children in the group want to contribute.

What happens in a discussion?

Many classroom discussions are dominated by the one person who is most experienced at discussion (the teacher), allowing only a very limited role to those who need most development. These so called 'discussions' are often no more than a series of dialogues between two individuals, the teacher and a child. Thus the teacher asks a child a question (often in the Socratic style of proof-by-intimidation) and the child responds. Once one child has responded a number of times, the teacher moves the 'discussion' on by focusing on another child, and for the next few moments it is his turn to participate.

This way of organising a discussion is often seen more clearly by the children than the teacher. They perceive classroom discussions as the teacher talking to just one child at a time. Moreover, the model of education that many children (and not a few adults) hold is that 'the teacher knows' whatever has to be known: the corollary of this is that 'children do not know'. Therefore, the argument goes that children only need to listen to the teacher because nothing any other child says has any value.

Clearly, in any useful discussion it is important that everyone listens to everyone else's views. Only listening to and accepting the teacher's utterances does rather limit the discussion! One useful way to show children that they need to listen to each other is the echoing technique. If you frequently (but not pedantically) repeat what a child has said, for example

'Thank you, Sarah, that was a very interesting point you made. What you're saying is that.... Now, who would like to say something about Sarah's point?' – four things can follow.
• When the teacher repeats the child's comment, the rest of the children actually hear it.
• By repeating it, the teacher shows that children's comments are interesting and valuable (though not necessarily correct or to be agreed with).
• The teacher can, to an extent, edit the discussion by highlighting the points that are likely to carry discussion forward and help create focal

points and structures for the discussion.

• The teacher can also sometimes rephrase a child's statement to make a point more economically and in a more focused and effective way. Not only does this help the other children, but it also provides a model against which children will build their further comments.

When it becomes clear to children that a discussion is more than a 'two-people-at-a-time' dialogue, another problem can arise. Since discussions are for all, everyone tries to speak at the same time. It is not surprising that children initially find it difficult to wait their turn. Several techniques may help.

• Tape-record instances when several members of the class speak at once and ask the group, when you play back the tape, if they can understand what's being said.

• Stop the discussion and talk about this problem. What solutions do the children have?

• Have some symbol or talisman that empowers the holder to speak: in *The Lord of the Flies* by William Golding (Faber & Faber) the children used a conch shell and only the child holding it could speak.

• Encourage the children to use gestures and eye-catching to indicate to the chair that they want to speak rather than waving their hands in the air or calling out to attract everyone's attention.

Fine judgements are made by people in a discussion: for example, a person who is speaking will have to decide whether to give way to another person who may be indicating that she wants to interrupt. Sometimes it can be right to allow someone to interrupt, sometimes it is less clear and sometimes it's best if the speaker can finish her point first. Equally, it is a matter of judgement as to whether or not to interrupt a speaker and if so, when. For example, it can be sensible to interrupt if you have some vital information that will change or modify the speaker's line of argument.

Discussion develops fine listening skills. It is a poor discussion in which individual contributions don't properly relate to points other speakers have made, and children need to be encouraged not just to listen to each other, but to rethink what they want to contribute in view of what has been said. Can they use someone else's points as a way of introducing their own? Does some previous contribution need to be extended, modified or refuted? This can only be done by carefully listening and thinking about what has been said in the light of one's own ideas.

Who should control the discussion?

Children will readily grasp the idea of someone chairing a discussion, and the term can be usefully introduced even

with very young children. You may, as teacher, want to chair discussions at the beginning, but if you present yourself very carefully as a role-model, and talk about how you are acting to chair the meeting ('I wonder if you could wait for a moment there, Peter, because I think Rani has a point she wants to make on that...'), it will very soon become possible to pass on the role of chairing a discussion to the children.

How do we organise a discussion?

The physical layout of a discussion group can have a great influence on its success.

If at all possible, each child should be able to see the face of everyone else participating in the discussion. With large groups, or the whole class, this will probably mean sitting in a circle and it is usually worth the effort of rearranging the classroom furniture to do this. Smaller groups can often work perfectly well when seated around a table. Being able to see each other means that children can begin to 'read' the facial expressions and body language of other members of the group. This makes it easier for someone to signal that they want to speak and avoids the unnatural hand-waving that can detract from thought. It is worth encouraging children to use minimal gestures to catch the eye of the chair or of the speaker – a finger will do – and to encourage the idea that once the gesture has been seen by either the speaker or chair, it is

acknowledged with a slight nod, so that the finger can go down. A sub-dialogue carried out in this way only minimally interferes with everyone following the spoken dialogue.

One way to extend this further is for the chair to make a short list of the order in which children indicate their wish to speak; the teacher might say, 'Right, Mary next, then Jake, then Manjula'. This establishes a queue, which means that Jake and Manjula know they have been seen and acknowledged (and can stop trying to catch the teacher's eye), and that others who later decide that they want to make a point know that the best moment to catch the teacher's attention will be after Manjula speaks.

As the chair of a discussion, you will be making a great many decisions in a short space of time, such as who to allow to speak and when, what points to encourage and which ideas not to follow up. In terms of the content of a discussion, it is inevitable that a selection is made, and the chair has to weigh up a number of factors in deciding how he is going to let the subject move on.

• What are the children as a whole interested in, and what do they have experience of?

• Which minority viewpoints must be included?

• Which points are off the main subject?

It can be worthwhile noting the points that are not followed up and use them as subjects for subsequent discussions.

Monitoring discussion: reflecting on practice

The activities suggested in this chapter provide a framework for developing skills. If several of the ideas are used together a programme of teaching can be drawn up. Such a programme will be greatly strengthened if you can find the time to monitor how the children's discussion skills are developing. It is possible, though difficult, to track the progress of these skills during a discussion – noting who speaks and when, how well each speaker links her contribution to other people's points, how she gains attention and so on – but it is usually easier to evaluate these factors through listening to a tape recording of the discussion. Another way, having a colleague sitting in to monitor a discussion, is a luxury few schools will be able to afford!

One factor that is particularly worthwhile monitoring is the gender balance in a discussion. It often happens that boys dominate discussions. This is generally not because they have any better or more useful contributions to make, but because often teachers allow boys to be more assertive in discussions as a way of keeping control. For example, letting them speak when they like may avoid disruption. If you notice that you are allowing a disproportionate number of boys to speak, it can be useful to point this out to the class and to impose, for a while, a restriction on the number of speakers from the boys in order to give the girls a chance. Such behaviour modification can be quite effective and the need for a teacher-imposed quota can, after a while, be dropped.

Learning to collaborate

The activities in this section explore ways of getting the children to act collaboratively in their discussions. These activities can be introduced in any kind or level of discussion, and will help sharpen skills of collaboration while focusing on children's talk. Each is a response to a particular kind of problem that you may find with your class in discussions.

• *Problem*: Every child wants to speak at the same time.
Solution: Activity 1 – Taking turns: the conch shell game.

• *Problem*: Children's contributions are interrupted by others waving their arms and calling out to speak next.
Solution: Activity 2 – Signals in discussion.

• *Problem*: Discussions meander all over the place – nothing any speaker says develops further anything that has been said before.
Solution: Activity 3 – The following-on game.

1. Taking turns: the conch shell game

Age range
Five to eleven.

Group size
Groups of six to the whole class.

What you need
A distinctive, easily grasped object such as a conch shell or a roll of adhesive tape.

What to do
Group or class discussions can be spoiled by a clamour of children wanting to speak at the same time, often waving an arm to attract attention.

the children a few examples of this to begin with.

This activity makes the children listen very carefully to what the others are saying, and also means that they have to establish very quickly a way of linking their own ideas to that of the last speaker. To do this, they will need to identify some of the key points made and either refute them, modify them or add to them as a lead-in to their own points. Some children will be able to begin by doing this and then turn the discussion in a different direction.

Further activity
Talk with the children about how much better and more satisfying their discussions are when they can develop each other's ideas. They will very quickly recognise the advantages, and the 'game' can then be dropped. Clearly, it isn't essential that every speaker in a discussion develops ideas from other contributions, but if the majority do this, there is a great gain in overall coherence.

Small groups, large groups

The activities in this section explore ways in which small groups and large groups can interact in a discussion. They can be adapted to be useful across the primary age range.

4. Small group talk

Age range
Five to eleven.

Group size
Groups of three to six.

What you need
No special requirements.

What to do
It is easier to begin to develop discussion skills when the children are organised in small groups. It may be best to begin working with one group at a time, while the rest of the class are engaged in some task that does not require so much of your attention, as once several groups begin to work at the same time it is impossible to monitor them all.

Try, as much as possible, to keep the children in the same groups, particularly in the early stages. Children will develop skills more quickly if they are secure in a group and know how different members of the group might respond. It is important, therefore, to select these initial groups carefully: as a general rule, one might suggest selecting groups in which every child has at least one friend, and at the same time ensure that each group contains, where possible, a mix of children by sex, ethnic background and ability. As skills develop and children gain in confidence, the stability of groups becomes less important – indeed, it becomes useful to encourage impromptu groups that vary in membership.

In small groups, children need at first to be encouraged to express ideas and opinions, and to realise that they are not being asked for 'right' answers. You might begin by asking open-ended questions, which have several possible responses and are therefore more likely to get things going than closed questions, with only one correct answer. As a very rough rule, questions that begin with 'why' and 'how' are more likely to be open-ended than those beginning with 'where', 'when', 'who' and 'what'.

Try at first to accept all answers as being helpful: offer praise for contributions and follow up short answers with supplementaries that ask for the child's opinion. Throw answers back at the rest of the group: do they all agree with the response given? Are there any other possible answers?

Don't let the first couple of discussion sessions last too long. Ten minutes may be quite long enough. After this, most children in a group will begin to take on more of your questioning role themselves, directly responding to each other's answers. At this stage, you will be able to begin to withdraw from the group, only coming back to collect their conclusions. Soon it will be possible to have several groups working in parallel, with you moving from group to group.

Further activity

Once small groups become established and confident in their ability to manage a discussion on their own, you will need to consider how you can extend these skills so that individuals are able to deal with larger and more diverse groups. The first stage in doing this may be to encourage groups to report to each other. Some of the ideas in Chapter 1, such as Activity 7 on page 25, may be useful here.

5. Small groups feeding into large groups

Age range
Five to eleven.

Group size
Several groups of up to six, then the whole class.

What you need
No special requirements.

What to do

Encourage the different groups of children to discuss independently aspects of the same topic. Then ask each group to select one member to report to the other groups on what the rest of their group thought.

Call the class together: it may be helpful to rearrange the seating so that all the children can see each other. Ask the representative of each group to report in turn and then allow members of the other groups to ask questions about what they have heard.

It is quite common for different groups to come to different conclusions, and this can lead to a good exchange of views between groups. Older children can sometimes become fixed to 'their' group's position, and defend this against the views of others. With younger children, you may find that the child selected to report the group's views instead substitutes his own views. This leads to other members of the group contradicting their representative. Encouraging them to do so helps develop the idea of accurate reporting of the group's views.

Further activity

Expanding the size of the discussion group in this way gives children the opportunity to gradually develop their discussion skills in a larger group. When they are accustomed to this, it becomes possible to introduce discussions directly to the whole class. This has the advantage of being quicker and more direct, and allowing at once the sharing of a much broader range of views. On the other hand, there is less opportunity for each child to speak. You will need to keep a balance between your different objectives.

Giving structure to the discussion

The activities in this section consider how children can learn to give effective structures to a discussion. Structure is needed so that everyone gets a chance to express ideas and opinions, so that views can be explored or challenged and so that a conclusion can be reached, if this is appropriate.

6. Gathering the views

Age range
Seven to eleven.

Group size
Small groups, up to the whole class.

What you need
Flip-chart and marker or blackboard and chalk.

What to do
In the early stages of any discussion, it is useful if the members of the group can get some measure of the range of experiences and views that are represented across their membership. Working with each group in turn, ask each member to begin by giving their initial ideas. Use a flip-chart or blackboard to note down the key experiences and/or views. When all the group members have reported, ask them all to look at the range that is represented. Can they see people who have similar and different ideas? Has every idea been represented? What are the main areas that it now seems important to discuss?

This sort of initial warming-up experience can help children develop a number of useful attitudes:
• not making initial statements that are too dogmatic or may offend others;
• understanding the usefulness of getting the early 'feel' of a group;
• giving everyone the chance and the confidence to have a say;
• understanding how to generate some sort of structure for the rest of the discussion.

The next time you ask the children to do this ask one child to take on the note-making role. Some children may find it difficult to make brief notes of what is said and attempt to write down everything that is said. Show the group how to select the key words and to note only these.

This procedure will be useful in the early stages of discussion. As children become more adept, the need to make notes may pass.

7. Organising the arguments

Age range
Seven to eleven.

Group size
Small groups up to the whole class.

What you need
Flip-chart and marker or blackboard and chalk.

What to do
A well-organised discussion will cover several aspects of a subject, one after the other. There will need to be some initial exploration of the breadth of the subject and children's ideas and initial attitudes (see Activity 6, page 92), followed by a more detailed discussion on each of the main issues, ending with some concluding discussions on which ideas are now held or where some kind of conclusion is reached. The responsibility for taking on this organisation usually lies with the chair, but you can share the responsibility with the class and show them how it is done.

When the children are used to having their initial responses collected together on a flip-chart at the beginning of the discussion, introduce the idea of having a programme for the rest of the event. Stop the discussion momentarily and indicate on the flip-chart the major issues that seem to have been raised. Link together similar ideas and views on the chart. Then number each one and say that you want the class to discuss each in turn, in this order.

In the next class discussion, follow the same pattern, but ask the children to suggest the order in which to tackle the main ideas. As they get used to this, ask them why they have selected this particular order. They will begin to see that the order in which they discuss these sub-issues is important for the overall success of the discussion.

Finally, you might allow the children to begin to identify and categorise the issues being raised. This is a sophisticated skill, but within the range of many junior-aged children.

8. Challenging ideas

Age range
Seven to eleven.

Group size
Small groups, up to the whole class.

What you need
Flip-chart and marker or blackboard and chalk.

What to do
In many discussions, particularly but not only in controversial areas, children will have conflicting views. They will need to gain experience in articulating their

views when someone else is arguing against them.

Develop this activity when the group or class has well-established discussion skills. When an issue arises that is clearly going to divide opinion, stop the discussion for a while and divide the group into two (or more) groups, representing the main points of view. Give each group a few minutes to prepare their case, independently. Then reassemble the whole group and ask each group to present their arguments. Split the class again and ask each group to discuss and present their refutation of the other group's points. This may need to be developed, so that points made by each side are listed and numbered.

Encourage the children to think carefully about their own arguments and to organise them so that they can be presented to challenge those with opposing views. They will need to listen carefully, both to what other people think, and to what other people say about their own case. It may help to discuss how to make remarks that criticise someone's arguments without being rude, wounding or humiliating.

Further activity
Consider organising a class debate on an issue that is likely to cause disagreement. Activity 13 (see page 99) on debating may help.

9. Coming to a conclusion

Age range
Seven to eleven.

Group size
Small groups, up to the whole class.

What you need
No special requirements.

What to do
Not all discussions need to have a conclusion. There may be no dividing issue, or there may be no need to reach a consensus. However, there will

★The ayes have it!

be times when a decision must be reached: for example, when the class or group are considering an activity that they are going to undertake as a whole. It is therefore helpful if you can identify to the children, before the discussion begins, whether you expect a decision to be reached. Explain that while everyone can put their point of view, eventually there will be only one outcome and that everyone, whatever their preference, will have to accept and follow this. When organising these sorts of discussions, try to ensure that the minority groups are given plenty of opportunity to explain their objections to what the majority seem to want. Make sure also that the holders of the majority view listen to these points and actually answer them, rather than simply using their numbers to force their viewpoint through.

It can be useful sometimes to be very explicit about what you are doing in this. Explain that one of the functions of a discussion is to let different views be heard, so that everyone can consider alternatives and reassess their own views.

Forums for discussion

The activities in this section are intended to include discussion in class and school arrangements so that it forms a greater part of the curriculum.

10. Class council

Age range
Five to eleven.

Group size
The whole class.

What you need
No special requirements.

What to do
Some teachers are happy to allow children a degree of autonomy over how the classroom is organised and

run. This can be achieved through a class council, where either the whole class or representatives meet regularly to discuss how the class operates, looking at the rules, the organisation of activities and suggesting improvements.

A whole-class council can be a good way to begin. Although it is likely to be more time-consuming, more repetitive and less precise in its discussion than a small council, it has the advantage of allowing everyone to participate directly. The alternative, which may be suggested by the children themselves if they find the whole-class proceedings too unwieldy, is for the children to

select a small group of representatives. Generally, one child per group of six is a useful ratio, but it will depend on the 'natural constituencies' into which your class is divided. It is probably best not to go for separate representatives of the girls and the boys, although you should ensure that both sexes are adequately represented.

Try to hold regular meetings: once a week works well for younger children and may do so for older ones if the meetings are kept short and snappy. Keep a public list of ideas for discussion that you and the children can add to during the week. You can then select a short agenda of items

from this list the day before the meeting. You may want to have a set of ground rules, such as no discussion of the behaviour of individual children or particular staff.

If your class has chosen representatives, instead of having a whole class council, you will need to allow some time before the meeting for them to collect the other children's views and find some way to announce decisions after the meeting.

Things that I have found class councils to have discussed successfully include:
• rotas for clearing up painting equipment;
• lining up;
• rules for the corridor;
• how birthdays should (and should not) be celebrated in class;
• finding time for quiet reading;
• giving boys and girls equal access to the computer.

Further activity
If class councils are a success in your school, the school may want to consider setting up a school council (see Activity 11 below).

11. School council

Age range
Five to eleven.

Group size
This normally involves between two and three representatives from each class in the school, but they will need to consult and report back to their own classes.

What you need
No special requirements.

What to do
Involving children in making decisions about the way that aspects of the school are organised can be an important part of the cross-curricular theme of citizenship (see the National Curriculum Council's

Curriculum Guidance 8: Education for Citizenship [1990] NCC). A school council can provide a regular forum for children to express their views and to participate in the running of the school.

The idea of a school council will need to be discussed thoroughly by the head, staff and governing body before it is established. The purposes and limits of its powers of discussion must be fixed and made very clear to all the adults working in the school and to parents, as well as to the children.

Some school councils discuss items such as playground rules, behaviour in corridor and lavatory areas and litter. Others also concern themselves with the general environment of the school, perhaps making decisions on the kind of play equipment that would be most useful.

Most school councils in primary schools are based on the class representative system, where the children in each class elect one or two children to represent them. Often the reception classes are not represented until the children in them have been in school a couple of terms, but most schools find that Year 1 and Year 2 children can handle the idea and practice of elections quite satisfactorily. Teachers of older children often note that their classes are sufficiently sophisticated to choose the children best able to collect and represent views, rather than simply the most popular children.

Meetings need to be held at least fortnightly. If they are less frequent the younger children, in particular, find the processes too drawn out. The meetings need to be chaired and experience suggests that a teacher (not the head teacher) can do this best, particularly in the early stages. The chair will need to ensure that children do not refer to individuals – other children, teachers and other adults in the school – in a derogatory way. This way the children will learn how to make their points in a way that does not cause offence to individuals.

The experience of many schools is that the chair will also need to act as secretary and chief executive. It is useful to have a written record of the main points made at the meeting and to ensure that teachers and representatives get a chance to see this fairly soon after the meeting. The chair will also need to see that any decisions that are made are fairly quickly passed on for action. It is important, particularly for the younger children, to have had some

kind of response by their next meeting.

An agenda will need to be prepared for each meeting and sent round a little in advance. Try to keep the agenda as simple as possible (no 'matters arising' or 'AOB'!).

The class representatives will need time to discuss the agenda with their class before the meeting, and time to report back afterwards. It can help avoid misunderstandings in the reporting back stage if the chair's notes of the meeting are available.

12. Discussions with adults

Age range
Five to eleven.

Group size
Any size.

What you need
No special requirements.

What to do
Bringing adults other than teachers into the classroom to discuss matters with children can often add greatly to the quality of the children's talk and develop their confidence in talking. On many occasions, adults will be involved in interviews with children (see Chapter 6). Discussions differ from interviews in that there is a greater emphasis on the exchange of ideas and less on the extracting of information. Therefore, the adults involved in any such discussion will need to be briefed. You will need to explain that you want them to talk *with* the children and not *to* them; to ask them questions about their ideas as much as the children ask questions about theirs.

13. Debating

Age range
Nine to eleven.

Group size
The whole class, or even two classes.

What you need
No special requirements.

What to do
Debating can be seen as a formalised discussion, in which the topic is firmly fixed as a proposition. Speakers are selected so that those agreeing alternate with those

Should everyone have an equal wage?

disagreeing. Principal speakers introduce the main arguments on both sides and, at the conclusion of the debate, summarise the main points. A vote may be held at the end.

Older children in primary school who have experience of discussion may find this an interesting form of organisation. You will need to explain to them that a good debate happens when the speakers have prepared their arguments in advance, yet are able to modify what they actually say in the light of points made by other speakers. The proposer and the opposer of the motion will probably need some particular help in their preparation.

Topics for discussion need to be selected with sensitivity – but they also need the possibility of divergent viewpoints or controversy. The following brief list of 20 topics includes suggestions that I have found worked well with primary aged children, but it is only intended to be a stimulus. You will need to select items that seem suitable for your class and, naturally, to modify the language to make it appropriate for the age of the

children. However, most areas for discussion will arise naturally from the curriculum you have selected, and so try to identify areas within these topics that will provoke a lively exchange of views.
• Are women better at certain jobs than men?
• Are boys more aggressive than girls?
• Should a woman's place be in the home?
• Should the very rich be taxed to help the very poor?
• What would be an ideal society?
• How should better-off countries help less well-off countries?
• Why should we try to prevent pollution and rubbish building up?
• What can we do if materials like oil begin to run out?
• How much are we prepared to do to keep the air clean?
• Does it matter if some types of animals or plants die out?

• Is meat-eating wrong?
• Should animals be used in medical research?
• Should everyone have an equal wage?
• Should there be stronger laws to stop people smoking?
• How can vandalism be stopped?
• Where should the class go for an end-of-year outing?
• How should the class set up a mini-enterprise?
• Plan, cost and carry through the organisation of a picnic.
• Are motor cars more of a problem than a help?
• Do we watch too much television?

CHAPTER 6

Interviewers

Getting information from another person is not simply a matter of asking questions, although this clearly plays an essential part. To conduct an interview calls for a subtle interaction with the interviewee – listening carefully to his responses, reading his body language, judging when to persist and when to let an issue drop, framing questions in a way that is direct, clear and precise, yet likely to achieve a useful response. The skills needed sound formidable, yet children in primary schools are able to begin to develop them, if they are given the contexts in which to work.

Interview techniques

How do children learn to frame questions? How can they be helped to listen to answers and to respond in an interactive way to the person they are talking to? The activities in this chapter are intended to develop these skills and explore the ways in which they can be practised and extended.

Providing opportunities for children to talk with adults other than teachers is a very useful way of helping them to understand how people work together, and a series of activities on this topic suggests ways to use adults in a variety of curricular areas. Children need to become aware of the needs and viewpoints of other people, and this calls for the development of particular qualities and skills in talking and listening.

One type of interview often found in magazines is the questionnaire, which is usually given to a celebrity. The result is a list of questions and answers that may read rather like this:
• What is your favourite colour?
Red.
• What is your favourite food?
Bananas.
• Which book has influenced your life most?
Paddington Bear.
• What is your zodiac sign?
Aries.
• Who do you talk to most?
My accountant....

A questionnaire like this, however, reveals virtually nothing about the person being interviewed. In this example, there is perhaps a hint of facetiousness in the last answer, although it could be caused by boredom with the questioner or perhaps even honesty. But we will never know, because the questioner has now inexorably moved on to ask about the celebrity's favourite flower or record or drink.

Quite a few children's first attempts at interviewing are rather like this unremitting

stream of data-gathering. Most adults move on to conduct a more satisfying form of interview, compilers of questionnaires excepted! But why do groups of children, when they are interviewing adults, so often start in this unpromising and unsatisfactory way? Firstly, there is a tendency for the children who are sharing the task of interviewing to see it as simply a turn-taking task. Therefore, each child prepares her own set of questions and asks them without reference to the questions asked by other members of the group. This can even lead to a child

reiterating a question which has already been asked by another child: it is not that she wasn't listening, it is simply that she feels that that was 'his' question and this is 'my' question.

Often an individual child will feel that he has to ask his own questions and listen to the answers to these, but those that someone else asks are nothing to do with him. Thus children who are beginning to conduct interviews tend to save up their questions until it is 'their turn'.

There is also a tendency for children to be over-prepared. This means that if a child has prepared a list of questions, she will ask these, in the form and order that she has prepared, irrespective of anything the interviewee might say. Therefore, interesting or

ambiguous answers are passed by and questions sometimes go back over ground the interviewee has already covered in response to an earlier question. Also, many of the questions children ask in an interview tend to be very factual, eliciting short factual responses. These responses can be useful in certain cases, but not if one is doing any more than gathering details.

What is a good interview?

In a satisfactory interview – and even very young children are able to develop good interviewing skills – the questioners prepare for the interview by discussing the areas they want to cover. They predict the kind of information they expect the person they are interviewing to give, and when the interview time arrives, they listen carefully to everything that is said, so that they don't repeat what has been said before. They are

sensitive to what the interviewee is saying. If he says something that they don't expect to hear, they follow it up with appropriate questions. Has he misunderstood the question? Is he avoiding giving an answer? Are there more questions to ask that will help the interviewers to understand this new information better?

To reach this level of skill, children need to practise developing their strategies and tactics of interviewing. The activities in this chapter include games and exercises that focus on particular aspects of conducting an interview. These are intended to be only temporary devices, aimed at helping the children

to focus on particular aspects of an interview.

It is very helpful if children are given the opportunity to analyse the problems of interviews themselves. If they can see, for example, the problem of repetition or of not realising that they were expected to listen and can discuss this with each other and with you, it is much easier for them to adapt their techniques and develop accordingly. The activities can then be dropped, as they have served their purpose.

Setting up an interview

Children need to prepare for an interview – but they rarely need to prepare by writing out the questions that they intend to ask. Rather, they need to review between them what they already know about the

subject and to think about what the person they are about to interview might be able to tell them.

They might consider first the factual details that the interviewee might be able to tell them. Making a few notes about topics to be covered (not questions to ask) might help in this. Similarly, they might decide to find out particular opinions or ideas held by the interviewee.

If a group of children are conducting the interview, they should arrange beforehand who will begin the questioning and what sort of areas each of them will cover. It is usually a mistake to have a fixed rota of turns to ask questions – follow-up questions often come most naturally to the person who asked the original question.

When the interview starts, the children may want a record of what is said. It is very hard – even for an experienced reporter with shorthand skills – to conduct an interview and make a transcription at the same time. The children should either make a tape recording of what is said or rely on their memory. If a recording is made, you will need to ensure that the children know how the tape recorder operates.

Transcribing a tape after the event generally takes four to five times as long as the recording itself and this can be a great drawback if a written copy is needed. However, there are several alternatives.
• Simply use the tape as a reminder, to be played through to refresh the memory.
• With younger children, it may be possible to ask a class of older children to help them transcribe the tape.

• You could make copies of sections of the tape on different cassettes, so that with several tape recorders and headsets, several children can transcribe the interview at the same time.

A transcript is not, however, usually necessary. It is often more useful to ask all the children to make quick individual lists of all the points covered in the interview, immediately after it: between them, most items are usually included. Then ask each child to either write about one or two items from the list – you could specify which, to ensure that everything is covered – or to write about the three or four items which impressed them most. The latter approach emphasises that it is what the interviewer himself finds significant that is important, not the whole event.

Whom should they interview?

The selection of interviewees depends very much on what information is being sought. Usually, someone is selected because they have some particular experience to tell about. Parents are often very good people to talk about the local area, and grandparents too can usually provide a good historical dimension.

Interviews don't only have to happen in school time. Children can be asked to interview parents, relatives or next-door neighbours after school or at the weekend, and to bring the results to school with them the next day. There are usually also quite a few adults working around the school or visiting for various reasons. On one occasion, my headteacher had invited four or five fellow heads to visit the school as part of an INSET course he was following. I managed to get them all into my classroom to be

interviewed by groups of children about the organisation of their own schools! There are also likely to be plenty of people who live and work in the locality who could be invited for interview.

Those adults who are not used to working with children may need some briefing from you about what to expect before the interview – how many children will be involved, why they are doing it and what sort of answers to give. Try to emphasise that their own direct experiences will be far more interesting to the children than explanations of the broader context. Once a class of mine were interviewing people about their experiences as evacuees in the Second World War and one man insisted on beginning by attempting to explain European politics in the 1930s. The children found this hard to follow, but perked up considerably when he went on to describe the horror he had felt, as a nine-year-old city boy, on crossing a country field at night during the blackout – cows, cowpats and all!

Sometimes, in order to collect lots of facts for a project, the children will need to conduct a questionnaire-type interview. For example, they may wish to gather local opinion on a planning proposal. Older children, with careful preparation and supervision, are quite able to work in pairs, interviewing passers-by in the street. They will need to prepare and try out their questionnaire first and it is important to give them fairly strict instructions concerning where to stand (so that they are all well within your sight) and to ensure that the same person isn't asked twice. A class of children can very quickly collect a large mass of data to analyse in this way and using a microcomputer with a data-handling programme can be a useful way of sorting it out.

ACTIVITIES

Organising interviews

The activities in this section are intended to be used to develop the essential skills of interviewing, with activities and games that build up various aspects of technique.

1. Don't say no – and don't say yes!

Age range
Five to eleven.

Group size
Pairs.

What you need
A watch with a second hand.

What to do
Ask one child in the pair to question her partner for exactly one minute. The child being questioned must answer all the questions, but without using the words 'yes' or 'no'. You may need to act as a judge and/or timekeeper for this, or other children in the class may be able to take on these roles.

This game helps the children to develop skills of thinking quickly, asking questions and listening with some care and precision. Initial attempts will be halting, often rather repetitive and not very successful, but children will improve rapidly as they learn to ask more difficult questions and give more evasive answers.

The form of questioning that the questioners develop in this activity is that which requires only yes or no answers. These are in some ways the least revealing of answers (though this form of questioning is much used by lawyers in television dramas!). Getting the children to identify closed questions helps them to realise that open-ended questions are more revealing and also to see that sometimes an interviewee has to be 'pushed' to give a non-evasive answer! A discussion with the class may help clarify these ideas with them.

Further activity
Try other activities that help children identify closed and open-ended questions. For example, you could suggest a list of topics and ask pairs of children to devise one closed question and one open question about each.

2. Learning with your children

Age range
Five to eleven.

Group size
Any size.

What you need
No special requirements.

What to do
Children's questioning skills are closely modelled on those they see being employed by familiar adults. In school, there is a tendency to ask questions that are factual, testing the knowledge of the child being interviewed. Therefore, children have a natural tendency to ask these kinds of questions in an interview themselves. So whenever an opportunity arises, it is helpful to provide alternative models of questioning to children. When the class or a group of children are interviewing someone, there is no reason why you should not, at times, join in the questioning. This not only enables you to keep the interview on course – not missing important points, for example – but provides important learning experiences for the children.

• They see the way in which you ask questions, and will model their own questions on this.

• They begin to realise the range of ideas about which people can be questioned and the sorts of questions that are permissible.

• They realise that in asking questions *you* are also trying to find out information – that *you* are learning alongside them, and not simply testing the interviewee to see if she can give you the answers that you already know to be correct.

It is possible to be quite explicit about the fact that you are learning with the class. Putting yourself in the role of learner can help children with the uncertainty of conducting an interview – reassuring them that there is no set of correct questions that must be asked.

3. Learning about your children

Age range
Five to eleven.

Group size
Any size.

What you need
A tape recorder or paper and pencil, photocopiable page 178.

What to do
When a group of children in your class interview someone – a parent, a visitor, another child or even you – you could

occasionally make a record of who says what. You can then use this record to analyse the pattern of questions and help you decide what specific help is needed to develop skills.

There are several ways of analysing an interview:
• by recording who speaks by name;
• by checking the questions to find out which are open-ended or closed;
• by looking at the questions to see which seek factual information and which an opinion;
• by seeing whether each question relates to the previous question or answer, or whether it introduces a totally new topic;
• by comparing the length of questions and comments and relating them to the length of each answer.

You could use a check-list (see photocopiable page 178) that allows you to categorise each question, using a series of ticks, as the interview progresses. However, it is more accurate – though more time-consuming – to do this from a tape recording.

Analyse your findings. Do a few children dominate the discussion? Do the children ask questions that elicit good answers? Are they able to 'manage' the conversation, introducing and developing topics?

Further activity
Discuss your findings with the children. Present them non-judgementally as a series of observations about their interviewing. If some children have asked a series of closed questions, simply point this out and ask them why this is so, whether it is helpful and what they might do about it.

4. Girl talk, boy talk

Age range
Five to eleven.

Group size
Any size.

What you need
Paper, a pencil.

What to do
During an interview, record the gender of each child who speaks. Very often, it will be the boys who dominate the discussion, initiating most

questions, speaking the longest and controlling most of what is said.

Collect information to see if this is normally so in your class. Show the information to the children and ask them what they think about this. Is it fair? Why does it happen? How can things be made fairer?

Further activity

Develop some of the children's ideas. These may involve strict turn-taking (which they will find brings some other problems), or specific periods of the interview reserved for girls' questions.

5. 'Give me your answer, do'

Age range
Seven to eleven.

Group size
Pairs, moving into larger groups for discussion.

What you need
A blackboard and chalk or flip-chart and marker pens, paper, pens.

What to do
This activity explores with the children what happens if interviews are prepared in a limiting and prescribed way, and looks at the unsatisfactory results that such interviews can give. The learning takes place in the discussion that follows the 'work'.

Ask the children what sort of questions they might ask someone to find out about, for example, what they like and dislike, what they believe in, what sort of things they do and so on. List their suggestions on the board or a large sheet of paper. You should be collecting questions like:
• What is your favourite food?
• Which politician do you dislike most?
• What is your favourite book?
• What sport do you like most?

Try to get the children to avoid purely descriptive questions, such as those about hair colour, number of brothers and sisters and so on.

Divide the children into pairs and ask each child to interview his partner by asking the questions listed on the board and writing down the answers. (You may use a system of numbering, so that the questions don't have to be written out again.) The name of the child being interviewed should be written at the top of the sheet. Emphasise that the interview should be conducted in private, so that the answers aren't seen by anyone else in the class.

Collect in the interviews and gather the children together. Explain that they are now going to see how successful the interviews have been in discovering information. Select an interview and, without revealing the subject, read out the questions and answers. Ask the children if they can

Who do you think this is?

identify who the person is who gave these answers. Many of the class, if not most of them, will be incorrect or will make guesses. Repeat this with another interview and go on until you have convinced the group that it is very hard to identify an individual from this sort of information.

Ask the children what they do know about any one of the interviewees. Does the information they have collected help them to see how that child thinks and behaves? Why does this sort of interview reveal so very little?

The children should begin to suggest that the questions are not the right ones. They may suggest that the questions were too fixed and that they couldn't ask supplementary questions that came out of the answers, or they may simply suggest alternative questions. Discuss with them the limitations of questions that simply establish lists of information and of questionnaires that follow a strict format. Suggest that they think of alternative approaches.

Further activities
If alternative questions are suggested, you could list these and repeat the exercise. It is probable that the second round of interviews will be no more successful than the first.

6. Open question, closed question

Age range
Seven to eleven.

Group size
Large groups or, with older children, a whole class discussion might be possible.

What you need
A blackboard and chalk or flip-chart and pens.

What to do
Closed questions are those that only have one possible answer, while open questions have several possible answers, all of which may be correct.

Generally, open questions are more revealing than closed questions (although many of the questions in Activity 5 on page 110 are technically open). Helping children to identify questions that don't have right or wrong answers is important, because many of the questions they are asked in school are of the 'right or wrong' variety and are asked by teachers to test children's knowledge. If this is the main model that children get, then they will find it difficult to ask open-ended questions themselves.

It is probably best to use this activity before the children have to interview someone in connection with other work that they are doing. There are suggestions for areas to work on later in this chapter (see Activities 10 and 12, pages

114 and 117). Discuss with the class the kinds of questions that they might ask and help them to classify each suggestion as closed or open. What sort of answers do they expect to get from each?

Write down the questions that they suggest. It will help if you take on the role of the potential interviewee and give similar kinds of answers to those you expect will be given.

During an interview it may well be necessary to ask some closed questions to establish certain 'facts' about what the interviewee has done or knows about. Do these come better earlier or later in the interview? Do the open-ended questions depend in any way on the nature of the answers that have come before?

You could then interview one of the children, using the techniques that you have discussed with them. As part of this, you might ask the rest of the class to decide if each of your questions is closed or open-ended.

Further activity
Ask the children to try out their new skills in a real interview (see Activity 7 below).

7. Try it yourself

Age range
Seven to eleven.

Group size
Large groups of twelve, up to the whole class.

What you need
A person to interview about a subject that interests the class – perhaps a parent about their work, or an older person about life in the 1930s or 1940s. A tape recorder would also be very useful.

What to do
This activity should follow on from some of the earlier preparatory activities, particularly the 'Open question, closed question' session in Activity 6.

It is probably better to cover up the questions that the children will have prepared before the interview. If they simply read out prepared questions from the board, the interview will be constrained and less attention will be paid to the interviewee. Then, with the interviewee's permission, record what is said.

As the interview develops, try to keep track of the quality of the questions that the children ask. Are they open-ended or closed? Do they come in an order that develops themes or ideas? Do they establish factual details early on? Are interesting points that the interviewee raises left unexplored by the children?

After the interview, the children will probably want to work on the content of the interview – the information they have gathered. But at some point after this, ask the

children to focus on the interview itself. Play the tape back, stopping it at points where you can concentrate on the questions that they asked. Ask the children to classify the questions as before (see Activity 6 on page 111) and to comment on how they might have been phrased or ordered differently in order to have gathered more information.

8. Listening to the speaker

Age range
Seven to eleven.

Group size
Groups of six, up to the whole class.

What you need
Some helpful parents.

What to do
A good interviewer listens to what is being said and bases his questions on this, rather than reading from a previously prepared list. Ask the children to watch, for example, how presenters of television chat shows hardly ever refer to their notes.

Ask a group of children to prepare to interview a parent whom you have invited to visit the class. Perhaps the children might want to find out what school was like when the parent was young or about the parent's work. Ask the parent to be as surprising and unexpected as he can in his answers. Sit with the group and help them to compare what the interviewee says with what they expected to hear. Ask the children to think ahead about what the answers to their questions will be and then, if the actual answer differs from this, to ask more questions to find out why.

An interviewer usually expects to hear a particular answer, but she must listen very carefully, in case the answer she gets does not match the answer she expects. She can then follow up with more questions. Trying this out several times, children will find that it is more useful to prepare a list of topics than a list of precise questions.

9. Hard to get

Age range
Seven to eleven.

Group size
Groups of six and upwards.

What you need
A helpful parent or colleague.

What to do
Not all interviewees are helpful. It is not only politicians who seek to evade questions; some other adults are evasive too. They may feel that certain topics are inappropriate for primary-aged children or think that some things are not important and so censor them out of their answers or keep them private.

Children need to develop the confidence to gently probe their interviewee, to see if more information is forthcoming after an apparent evasion of an answer.

Brief the interviewee to answer questions on a particular topic – but to hold back some vital information that the children will need in order to make sense of the interview. Ask them to try to avoid referring to this, by stonewalling, missing the point or offering alternative answers. Ask the children to press, as delicately as possible, to find out as much as they can.

After the interview, discuss the tactics that were used by the interviewers and interviewee, with both parties concerned. Ask the children why they think a person might appear not to want to answer. Is this always acceptable? When and how can they judge when to go on asking? How can they do this without appearing rude?

Further activity
You might follow this activity with some court-room dramas, where the children can pretend to be barristers taking on 'hostile' witnesses. In this case they will have to probe very hard for a reply, but emphasise that most interviews cannot be taken to such lengths!

Questionnaires and their uses

The activities in this section provide useful suggestions and activities for interviewing lots of different people using a set of questions, and then how to analyse the results afterwards.

10. Just a list of questions?

Age range
Seven to eleven (this activity can be adapted for younger children).

Group size
The whole class, in pairs and small groups.

What you need
Paper, clipboards.

What to do
The questions asked in a questionnaire are different from those asked in an interview. The same questionnaires are usually given to a relatively large number of people, so that results can be collated and compared. It is therefore important to make sure that exactly the same questions are asked of all the people. Children often know about questionnaires from hearing about opinion polls.

Ask the children to construct a questionnaire to use with the public. There are many areas suitable for investigation, for example:

Are you male or female?

• people's occupations;
• their attitudes to this consumer-type survey;
• opinions on local transport;
• views on local conservation or amenities.

In almost every case, it will be very helpful to collect some background data on each person questioned, for example, their sex, approximate age, where they live and so on. This sort of information helps a great deal in the analysis of the rest of the data.

Get the children to try out their questions on each other and compare the results. They will quickly come to the conclusion that if they ask open-ended questions, they will be involved in quite a lot of writing, and this will be difficult if questioning a passer-by in the street. However, it is often possible to offer interviewees a choice of answers. Deciding on the categories of answers may limit the responses, but means that a tick can be put in a box, rather than a word or sentence written down.

Ask the class to pool their questions, so that a common set is agreed upon. You may need to discuss what questions are suitable. For example, it may not be sensible to ask people their age, but you could ask the children to estimate the interviewee's age in broad age bands. Children can be surprisingly accurate in these estimations. You may need to prompt them to include other background information – for example, the sex of the person questioned. (I once let my class discover the hard way that it wasn't actually necessary to ask passers-by if they were male or female!)

When the questionnaire has been agreed, make one good copy (type it if you can), including boxes to be ticked. Then make enough copies so that there is one for each person you intend to interview. If the class is not using a computer, it is easiest to collect exactly 50 or 100 or 200 questionnaire results.

Go into the street to collect people's responses. The children can work in twos or threes, and a busy street is best. Decide on a short stretch of road and position an adult helper at each end so that they can supervise the children. Ask the children to interview the people as they approach the area, from whichever direction, rather than as they leave, as this will avoid duplication.

Conduct the survey early in the day and make sure that you can see all the groups at

work. Remind the children to ask the people they stop if they are willing to be interviewed – the majority will be happy to help. A whole class working on a relatively busy street should be able to collect 100 to 200 responses in an hour.

Back in the classroom, ask the children to sort the results. If a computer is not being used, a simple tally chart can be constructed. Finally, discuss what the results mean.

11. Sorting it all out

Age range
Seven to eleven.

Group size
The whole class, working in groups of three to six.

What you need
A microcomputer (for a period of at least a week), and a data-handling program, such as *Grass*, *Key*, *Quest* or *Ourfacts*.

What to do
Using a data-sorting program enables the children to check their ideas quickly against the information that they have gathered (for example, do older men tend to have lollipops as their favourite sweet?). Although it takes some time to enter the data on the computer, much time is saved in sorting it and data can be searched again and again in a rapid and accurate way.

With the class, construct a data file, in much the same way as you would draw a table of results. What do the children think the heading for each column should be? What information will go in it? How much space will they need to allow for the information?

When all this has been decided the children can begin to enter the data. Groups of three children should spend half an hour entering data from the questionnaires and then another group can replace them. This saves a great deal of time and allows everyone to become familiar with the data.

Different groups can try out different hypotheses. It is likely that any one result will stimulate a large number of supplementary investigations.

Further activity
Ask the children to make graphs and charts to show their findings – some data handling programs will do this for them. What do the charts show?

Working with adults

The activities in this section suggest projects and curricular work in which children can use interviews to gather information.

12. Talking with adults

Age range
Five to eleven.

Group size
Any size.

What you need
No special requirements.

What to do
Allowing the children to work with 'real' people makes for a much more satisfying interview than practising on other children and teachers. There are many sources of people to interview.
• Parents are usually a good source for work on a variety of topics, such as childhood, work, local changes and so on.
• Grandparents are often not as accessible as parents, but are very good on history in the 1930s, 1940s and 1950s.

• Local workplaces are good for understanding the variety and organisation of work (see Activity 13 below).
• Contacting an old people's home or writing a letter to the local paper or to the social services can produce lots of older people willing to talk about the past. This can be good for the old people, as well as for the children!

Try wherever possible to prepare the interviewees beforehand. Explain what the children are doing, and how they are likely to question them. After the interview, try to give some sort of feed-back to the interviewee: tell him what the children have done and possibly get a child to send him a letter or a drawing.

13. A world of work

Age range
Five to eleven.

Group size
Any size.

What you need
Someone from a workplace – perhaps a parent, a police officer, a factory worker, a bank clerk, a shop-keeper and so on.

What to do
Ask the children to find out, through an interview, whether the interviewee likes her work; whom she works with; how the work is organised; how she got her job, and so on. The children will need to discuss the kinds of question they will ask, the order in which they will raise new areas and who will be responsible for each area of questioning.

Ask a series of people from different workplaces into the classroom, or ask several different people from the same workplace who do different jobs or have different responsibilities. The children should then compare the different perspectives.

Further activity
Organise a visit to the workplace so that the children can meet the interviewee on her own ground. Different groups could explore aspects of the workplace through

interviewing different workers – the organisation, where the money comes from, recruitment and training, work processes and changes in the workplace.

14. Ideas for change

Age range
Five to eleven.

Group size
Any size.

What you need
Adults willing to talk with children about current social issues.

What to do
Ask the children to find out how different people think that society could be improved. The children will have ideas of their own and these could form the basis of an initial group or class discussion (see Chapter 5). When they have decided what they think are the important issues, ask the children to discuss and compare their ideas with those of the visiting adult.

What do they think are the contemporary problems around them? They will probably be influenced by the media in their choice. What solutions are there? How can these begin to be implemented?

Further activity
Discuss other people's ideal societies. If the children are raising issues about the local amenities or services, invite in local councillors or council officials to hear the children's case and to respond.

15. Life history

Age range
Five to eleven.

Group size
Any size.

What you need
Some older people who are willing to recall past events in their lives with the children.

What to do
It may help when selecting interviews to target people with particular memories – for example, ex-pupils of the school or people who can remember being evacuated in the war. Helpers in the school can be a good source for suggesting contacts, as can the people in the records or archives section of your local library. Before the visitor comes in, help the children to establish a sense of the period on which you are concentrating. Use photographs, artefacts and local buildings to help in this. Discuss what life was like at that time. This will give the

children a framework against which to question their visitor. Ask the visitor to try, as far as possible, to talk about his own direct experiences.

Further activity

Ask the children to compare different people's memories of the same event. Do their stories vary? If so, why? Do the textbook accounts of the period or events match what people remember?

16. Transcribing the tapes

Age range

Seven to eleven.

Group size

Pairs.

What you need

Tape recorders – as many as possible!

What to do

Transcribing the tapes of an interview takes a long time, and is very laborious. If your class have made a recording of an interview that they feel is worth writing out, the following ideas might make it easier.

• Cut the tape into short, manageable pieces. You needn't literally cut the tape: if you have a tape recorder that will copy tapes, you could re-record short extracts from the original copy. Number each of the copied sections in order. Then you can give a relatively short piece to each pair of children to transcribe.

• With younger children's tapes, try involving a class of older children and asking them to do the transcribing.

17. Sorting the information

Age range

Seven to eleven.

Group size

Groups of four to six.

What you need

Notes or transcripts of an interview, coloured pens, card.

What to do

A written transcript of an interview can be quite difficult to use in class, particularly if it is long and in several different styles of handwriting. Ask a group of children to sort out notes so that they are easier to use. One way to do this is to stick the interview remarks on to a series of cards (numbered in sequence, so that the notes can be put back in the original order). Put a fresh idea on each card, so that the cards can be rearranged to bring together all the points on related themes.

Use coloured pens and some kind of coding system to identify the subjects and the information carried on each card. This can make it much faster to find what you want.

CHAPTER 7

Talking about the past

Recent history is a fruitful area for developing language skills, as children can act as historical investigators and talk to adults about their experiences. Oral history provides many valuable insights into the everyday life of ordinary people.

Many of the specific forms of talking and listening used in this chapter have been discussed in earlier chapters, particularly in Chapters 5 and 6. This chapter therefore simply offers suggestions for historical contexts in which to develop discussion and interviewing skills, and highlights specific strategies that have a part to play in the development of historical thinking and understanding.

Oral work in history is particularly important in the primary stage of schooling because it allows those children who are still finding it a struggle to develop reading and writing skills to develop as historians. If teachers are over-reliant on getting things written down, then the teaching and learning of history are dictated by the speed a child learns to write.

BACKGROUND

History provides several arenas for the development of oral skills. Oral history has already been mentioned as a means of obtaining source data. Role-play is an important way of helping young children to imagine how other people in other times might have felt and of synthesising their knowledge about the past with their imagination and feelings. Much historical work in schools demands discussion, as children collaboratively assess different points of view, and agree on interpretations and meanings.

History is seen by some as a difficult area within the primary school curriculum. It deals with matters in the past and it is assumed that children have difficulties in understanding the concept of historical time. History is based on incomplete evidence, which may confuse, and evidence which is often written in difficult handwriting or in foreign languages (or both). Some people believe history provides few examples of anything concrete on to which children can latch in their learning. But these are very negative views. It is possible to teach history in a lively way that helps children to grapple with problems of evidence, causality and chronology.

Talking and listening skills are important in this way of working. Three principal ways of exploring history through speaking and listening are explored in this chapter, oral history, role play and discussing evidence.

Most of these have suggestions to show how they might be located within specific units of history, and it should be possible to see how these approaches can, in many cases, be modified to help children explore any unit of history.

CONTEXTS

Oral history

Talking to other people about events in their past brings the past alive in a way that books and pictures are unable to do. Perhaps even more important, oral history provides a way of letting children handle real historical evidence at first hand. Hearing different accounts of the same period, children will discover that the versions do not always agree. This is important, because it means that they will have to find some way to account for the dissonance. They may offer explanations that revolve around faulty recollections, or they may suggest that the different views represent biases or points of view. Any of these explanations could be correct, and grappling with problems like this, even in the primary years, helps children understand the dependence of the historian on her fragile sources, and the tentative nature of the way in which we reconstruct the past.

Suggested approaches

Work in oral history can be suitable for anything from a small group to a whole class. The temptation, if a visitor is coming to talk to the school, is to cram in as many bodies as possible. However, it is probably better to have fewer children, so that a greater level of interaction can occur. If the visitor is prepared to do it, speaking to a third of the class

Nobody was very sympathetic!

Everyone in our village was right behind them all!

Can you remember the General Strike? If so would you like to visit Greenwood Primary School and tell us about your memories...?

at a time would usually be more productive. One successful pattern is for each group to work with the visitor on a different theme, so that when each group meets the visitor they spend their first few minutes establishing the basics (which may be repetitious for the visitor, but is short) and the greater part of the time in discussing the group's particular theme.

Selecting interviewees
There are a number of history study units which lend themselves well to oral history; for example, Britain since the 1930s, the local history units,

many of the supplementary units dealing with themes such as buildings, housing, education and so on, and much of the infant history curriculum. Decide what you want an interview to be about – school life in the past, the General Strike, evacuation or whatever, and then look for people who might be able to help with this. Calculate how old they will need to be to have memories of the period or event in question. Ask people that you know, or write to the local paper and try old people's clubs. Once you have found one person, she will often be able to lead you to her friends and contemporaries.

Suggestions for possible areas for interview (with different people) include:
• the General Strike;

• the coronation of Queen Elizabeth II;
• the first time I saw a television;
• going to school;
• cooking and washing at home.

Briefing
Brief your interviewee carefully. Tell him that you are particularly interested in his personal recollections – what he did and what he remembers, rather than what was in the news at the time.

Linking memories to a specific event may help tie down memories of home life such as cooking, recreation or schooling, to a particular date.

You will also need to brief your class. Give them some background information about the period or events that you think might trigger significant questions. Help the class decide their questioning strategy.

During the interview
Help the class with the interview. You will be learning

too, so make this obvious to the class and give them a model of how to ask good questions. Taking some photographs of the interviewee may help to remind the children of the event later, as will asking some of the children to draw pictures of the person during the interview.

Make sure that the interviewee is thanked properly. A letter from a child or a picture will often be greatly appreciated, as would a formal letter from the school.

Role-play

Oral history is limited to the human life-span, although it is possible to listen to recordings of people who died in the late nineteenth century. Role-play can allow children to move into the more distant past. Given a certain amount of information organised in a semi-structured way, children can create roles that allow them to understand the pressures on people in the past and why certain decisions were made.

Successful role-play will depend on the children being given sufficient background information – about contemporary materials and artefacts, the sort of person

they are to play, his relation to other characters and what has already happened before the role-play starts. They will then be able to add this information to their own understanding of human needs and aspirations. An initial discussion with the class about the possible perceptions and needs of people at the time in which the role-play is set will help establish this mood.

Through role-play and the debriefing that follows it, children can begin to appreciate the nature of historical causes.

Suggested approaches

It is possible to organise the class for role-play in several different ways:
• parallel groups, each working on the same themes at the same time;

• different groups, each representing a particular group of people and interacting with other groups to contribute to the whole picture;
• the whole class working together, with different roles for individuals as the drama unfolds.

Different historical scenarios and the different ages of children will determine which form of organisation is best.

Your role

You can also vary the degree to which you are involved yourself. It can sometimes help to take the role of a figure in authority, such as the village elder, the lord of the manor or the captain of the ship. This will allow you to take command of the story-line, introducing and contextualising new information for the children and keeping them in character. (For example, 'Have any of you crew members sighted land yet? Where do you think it might be?')

The stages of role-play

There is not always a great deal of acting needed in role-play. Much more of the time is taken up in talk and discussion. A typical role-play goes through several stages:
• The teacher briefs the class or group, describing the context, assigning roles and giving each group or character a specific task. These tasks could involve some kind of preparation, evaluation, stock-taking or planning – something that enables the children to think themselves into the role.
• The groups variously take on these tasks, discussing their activities and sometimes making necessary lists, programmes, timetables and so on.
• The teacher introduces some changed circumstances or brings together two or more groups with different perspectives and needs.
• The groups interact or consider the changes brought about, and then take on some new task that makes them reformulate the earlier pattern.
• The teacher introduces more changed circumstances, or brings together other combinations of groups, and so on.

Have any of you crew members sighted land yet?

Once the role-play has been completed you can organise a debriefing discussion, where the various groups explain to each other why they came to particular decisions and conclusions.

Suggestions for role-play
• The planting revolution: neolithic people change from being hunter-gatherers, on the move every few days, to growing crops. What are the consequences for settlements, refuse disposal, organisation, possessions and so on?
• Castle building: where should a castle be built? Why?

What materials are available? What other resources are needed? What will local people say about this?
• Medieval village justice: what rules does a small rural community need? Who will make them? What happens when someone appears to have broken a rule?
• Sea voyages: who is needed on a voyage of exploration? What do the people that they meet think of being 'discovered'? What kind of trade and bartering takes place?
• Moving to town: why did many country people move to towns in the nineteenth century? Were there pressures to move out of the country, or things in town that attracted people? What did it feel like to break away from one's roots?

Discussing evidence

History is based upon the evaluation of evidence from the past, and these evaluative processes take place initially through oral language. Much useful work can take place in primary classrooms through children discussing historical evidence in small groups. Contemporary illustrations and photographs of artefacts and remains can be used in most historical studies with young children. The evidence of contemporary written accounts is often less accessible for children, though there are collections available that could be read to the children or taped for them to follow.

The examples given below are drawn largely from the area of local history, because this is the area in which more organisation is needed to marshal resources.

The key questions that children should be encouraged

to ask when looking at any form of historical evidence are:
• What does this seem to tell us?
• Who made or wrote this?
• Where did it come from/who chose it and why?
• When was it written or made?
• What can we tell from it about the people who lived at this time?
• What else do we need to know or would we like to know?

Generally, there will be no clear-cut answer to questions such as these, so that real discussion and evaluation will be necessary. The techniques described in Chapter 5, and some of the group processes mentioned in the first chapter, will be useful in organising work in the classroom.

Suggested approaches

Historical evidence is rarely straightforward and uncontroversial, and when they are discussing significance and meaning children need to exercise real linguistic and historical skills. Most history books are secondary sources, and the evidence they contain has been preselected and predigested for the reader, very often with the writer's own interpretation included in such a way that it is hard to disentangle the evidence from the interpretation.

Pictures

Although a lot of evidence is hard to understand, there are many other kinds of evidence that are much more accessible. Contemporary pictures, for example, can tell children a great deal about life in the past. Occasionally, something like the Bayeux Tapestry can reveal an entire narrative account. But when looking at pictures, children need to ask why the picture was made. Whose viewpoint does it represent? What does it show and, just as importantly, what does it exclude?

Local history

Local historical evidence can be particularly useful, not only because it may be relevant to the everyday lives of the children themselves, but also because it is often relatively accessible. Local authority library services maintain archives of local historical resources, which are usually available for teachers to use with their children. Most such archives contain maps, photographs, census returns and street directories.

Maps

Make photocopies of a series of maps of the same area but dating from different times. It can sometimes help to decide to work only on a discrete local area and to trim down the maps to cover just this region (thus avoiding parts that might be distracting). Use the photocopier's enlarging facilities to produce large-scale maps using the same scale – this makes comparisons simpler, particularly if you have additional copies made on transparent acetate sheets. Many LEAs also have licence agreements to allow copies to be made of Ordnance Survey maps, to allow comparison with the present.

Photographs

Photographs of your area in the past – even the very recent past – can be used to explore ideas of change. With the archivist's permission, copy photographs for school use – use a reasonable quality camera to photograph the original, ensuring that it is held steady in a well-lit position. Have the photographs enlarged as big as your school can afford, and take them with you when you take the children to stand on the same spot as the photographer stood. What is different? What is the same?

Census returns

The records made by census enumerators become available a hundred years after the census was taken. They will list who lived in each household – their names, ages, occupations, relationships, birthplaces and more. This can be a very interesting way for junior aged children to find out about life in the nineteenth century. They could explore the history of a street or even their own house. They could use a data-handling program on the microcomputer to store, sort and analyse the information.

Street directories

In many places, these were published every year (unlike the ten-yearly census counts). Though the information is usually confined to a single name for each address, it is possible to trace how a building changed occupancy over long periods of time. Shopping streets in particular give very interesting findings on change and continuity – owners changing, types of business staying constant – over many decades. If looking at every year is too daunting, try sampling every third or fifth year.

CHAPTER 8

Talking mathematics

There are two main reasons why children talk: to communicate with others and when talking to themselves. To this can be added a third reason specific to learning, talking so that the teacher can have an insight into the way a child is thinking. These reasons have a particular cogency in the way children learn mathematics in the primary school.

Mathematics is sometimes seen as another language, with its own specific symbols and rules. This is only true to a limited extent. Mathematics is used in everyday life and has a natural relationship with everyday language. Mathematics is also learned through language – from the nursery rhyme jingle 'One, two, buckle my shoe', onwards.

Talking and listening are particularly important in learning mathematics.

Teachers' mathematical explanations are in most cases spoken, as are children's questions, queries and explanations. When children are able to articulate their difficulties in learning mathematics, we are given an insight into how they are thinking about and interpreting mathematical concepts.

BACKGROUND

There are a number of ways in which talking provides modes of learning for mathematics. The Non-Statutory Guidance for mathematics lists:
• describing;
• explaining;
• clarifying ideas;
• giving examples;
• making predictions;
• asking questions;
• reporting outcomes;
• talking through difficulties;
• discussing with peers.

The Cockcroft Report (*Mathematics Counts*, HMSO, 1982) made even greater claims for the need for oral language in learning and teaching mathematics. It notes that children often had difficulties in seeing the relationships between all the varied aspects of mathematics. The report suggested that 'the many different topics... within mathematics... should be presented and developed in such a way that they are seen to be inter-related. Pupils need the explicit help, *which can only be given by extended discussion*, to establish these relationships; even pupils whose mathematical attainment is high do not easily do this for themselves' (paragraph 246: my italics).

The mathematical activities that spark off this kind of discussion and talk will require a very different environment from the mathematics classroom in which children are all learning individually, at their own pace, from a book. The only talk here will be between individual children and the teacher when their work is discussed. Talk will not take place when children are all working on written problems. Children will need to be grouped and given problems that need to be solved by working together as a group. Such problems must be meaningful, giving rise to conjecture and hypothesis, not just empty exercises. Some suggestions for approaches

that develop these sort of problems follow on pages 134 to 137.

Mathematic talk

All mathematical learning in the primary school will be mediated through language – in teachers' and children's explanations of what they are doing, how, and what it means. Only the most routine of exercises will not require talk, and even these will need discussion when explanation is required.

A degree of accuracy in verbal descriptions is necessary in order to emphasise the correct meaning. For example, it is easy to refer to the digit seven in the number 174 as 'seven', rather than 'seven tens', or 'seventy', or even 'the digit seven'. But a child at a certain age of development or confusion, hearing it referred to as 'seven', may interpret the digit in this context as referring to the number seven, and become hopelessly confused. It isn't an easy area; we may talk of the number 'one thousand and sixty-six', yet the same figure in history becomes 'ten sixty-six'. Both are 'correct', but both are likely to cause some confusion.

In any mathematical work children need to be explicitly encouraged to explain to their peers or to the teacher what they are doing. The explanation can be concerned with methods of tackling a problem, techniques for solving a computation, or describing what has been discovered through a mathematical investigation. Whatever it is, explaining what they have found forces the learning experience and makes children think considerably more clearly than if their task was merely putting something down on paper.

Writing down a figure can be a private act, designed to put an end to a matter that may not be fully understood. Explaining something helps bring misconceptions to the fore and allows a dialogue in which children can have difficulties explained to them. This in itself is much less threatening than an irrevocable mark in an exercise book.

Approaches for using talk

The following suggestions cover a wide range of mathematical skills and areas – from handling information and displaying data to computational skills. Although many activities are concentrated in a few specific areas of mathematics, they will all involve some work in other areas. It is essential that the links between the various areas are seen and understood by the children, not only so that they are aware of the scope and unity of mathematics as a whole, but also so that learning in one area can buttress and support learning in another area.

Speculation and hypotheses

When children collect information, it is not always easy for them to classify and sort it because of the number and complexity of the items involved. This may mean that information collected is not used to its full potential. For example, traffic survey data may simply result in some bar-charts showing the comparative number of buses, cars and lorries, although it may be possible to link this information to time, direction, speed, weather and other factors. Information-handling and display lend themselves to collaborative work, from agreeing the design of the data collection, through the gathering and analysis, to the eventual communication of findings. All these activities are bounded by questions that need to be discussed.

• What do we want to show?
• What do we mean by this?
• How can we demonstrate it?
• What information must we collect?
• What shall we compare?
• What do we think the links will be?

These questions all relate to the hypothetical mode of enquiry, when children (and adults) make some guesses as to what might be connected and then explore, through testing or data collection, whether the guess can be disproved.

Using information-handling programs on a computer can help children do this better and give greatly increased opportunities for children to talk to each other as they

hypothesise, compare and explain their findings.

Children can collect data from:
• scientific experiments – such as timing the speeds of different weighted cars on a sloping surface, or testing the ability to hear certain noises;
• environmental surveys – the location and density of particular plants in a locality, or of animals, or of traffic levels;
• historical sources – such as census returns (see Chapter 7);
• social surveys – such as different languages spoken in the school, dietary preferences, or people's opinions.

If the collection of data involves asking people questions, see Chapter 6, which gives some useful guidance on questionnaire design.

Talking and information-handling

Children will need to discuss what they hope to find as they design their survey. They will need to decide what information to collect, and to create a field for each piece of information. For example, if a class wished to collect information on children's languages, then they might want to record for each individual the following information:
• name;
• class;
• age;
• sex;
• mother's first language;
• father's first language;
• child's first language;
• child's second language;
• child's third language;
• child's first written language....

Deciding what to collect will provoke lots of discussion. Do we really need to collect the person's age? Do we need information on which languages are spoken and written or only on spoken languages?

When they have decided what to collect, the organisation of the data-gathering may require more talk from children. The inputting of the data on to the

microcomputer will not require much discussion, but devising questions to extract relationships from the data will initiate an enormous amount of purposeful discussion. It may help to set groups of four or five children particular areas to investigate. Ask each group to prepare their own questions, to use the micro and then to decide how best to display their findings. Very often, the results of one investigation will set off fresh questions to be followed up.

Experimentation and testing

When children use sets of construction materials to make models, they explore qualities of shape, size, scale and relationships. Working in groups of no more than four, a great deal of useful discussion can develop as children work together to solve problems. The talk that emerges is valuable in helping them give precision to their communications, as well as developing and using a wide vocabulary concerning relationships, shapes, sizes, position and direction.

If the task encourages experimentation and testing in small groups, the need to communicate effectively will be that much more important. Questions that encourage discussion will tend to begin like this:
• How do you think you can make...?
• Could you explain how you would go about...?
• What do you need to know if you want to...?

• Why did you...?
• What do you think would happen if...?

Manipulating and measuring

When small groups are making models collaboratively they need to discuss what they are doing all the time. Much of this talk can be channelled in mathematical directions. The teacher will need to decide on a level of task appropriate to the group's mathematical needs.
• Younger children's talk might focus on simple size and relationship descriptions of the junk model that they are making: 'It's not big enough', 'That one's smaller', 'Put it behind/over/next to...'.
• Older children may be using language that includes descriptions of shapes in assembling a model from waste materials: 'The red cuboid', 'Cut a rectangular piece', 'Let's put half-circles here'.

• Children who are older still may be considering accurate measurements in their discussions; 'I need three struts that are 35 millimetres long', 'Try it about a centimetre wider', 'I think it needs to be much heavier – try another 50 grams'.

Much of the mathematical talk will be determined by the setting of the task. The direction of the language may need to be set off partly by the teacher, in asking sufficiently pointed questions at the outset, and by using the appropriate vocabulary and descriptions within the group.

Planning and organising

Any task that involves planning a group activity will necessitate talk and discussion. If the task also involves mathematical skills, then the talk will also include mathematical talk. For example, if a group of children are asked to plan for a class outing, this could include discussions on:

• cost – how much is available, what transport will cost, what else will need to be purchased, and so on;

• times – what time buses or trains leave, time taken on travelling, when it will be necessary to start packing up, leaving times and so on;

• distances and routes – using maps, interpreting scales, checking directions;

• calculations – cost of the outing per child, sums required for group bus or train tickets and so on.

Another planning activity might centre around a designing and making problem. Given the task of making something within certain constraints (of cost, weight, size or any other factor that involves mathematics), a group will need to use that constraint in their discussion and planning.

Designing and meeting needs

Activities that involve design and display can often contain a mathematical element. When such activities are carried out by small groups, there will inevitably be mathematical language in use.

• Selecting kitchen units from a catalogue, to fit a given space for example, will result in careful discussion about priorities and about size and cost.

• Looking at floor patterning and tiles will give rise to discussions about area and tessellation.

• Making class or group books involves estimating the size of what will be included, calculating sizes, measuring pages and covers and so on.

CHAPTER 9

It's only make-believe

Play is a talk-centred activity that fosters children's confidence in talking and listening in a wide variety of contexts. In the infant class, and in many junior classes, play can be seen as an essential context for learning. The home corner is a very important area of the classroom in which roles can be taken on and explored, and in which ideas about the meaning of words, the structure of sentences and the use of language can be tested with confidence.

This chapter sets out some of the play contexts in which speaking and listening can be organised.

BACKGROUND

Although they are only set out briefly here, the ideas in this chapter are central to the development of spoken language in the early years curriculum. However, the ideas are not only directed at the reception and infant class teacher: many of the contexts described here can profitably be used with children up to lower secondary level. Clearly, the language and the content will change as children mature and gather wider experiences, but the play context remains a useful one in which ideas can be explored and tested.

I once established a role-play bank in my Year 6 class. The basic theme for the role-play was a group of would-be entrepreneurs trying to start a small clothes-making business, for which they would need the help of the bank. The clothes-makers and the bank officers brought in their respective advisers and specialists to demonstrate the depth of the research that had been put into testing the financial viability of the proposal. This enormously interesting project followed several visits by the children to a local branch and a survey of 150 passers-by about their opinions of banks. The children not only dropped into role with alacrity, but took on the vocabulary and mannerisms of the people that had been working at the bank. One girl found herself suddenly cast in the role of the bank manager being asked for an overdraft. She leaned forward and peered over the

top of her glasses: 'Exactly what are you offering in the way of collateral to secure this loan?' she asked.

The place of play

The theory of learning through play has its roots in the work of Montessori, and the practice is not simply a matter of leaving children to themselves. The contexts for play need to be carefully selected and structured in order to maximise the learning possibilities. Play is *not* an alternative to 'work' – play *is* a young child's work. It is ironic that in the past some teachers saw play as an afternoon activity option for children who had completed their work. Those children least able to complete their formal work – and thus in most need of the enactive learning that takes place through play – were thus those least likely to ever get an opportunity to play.

Play needs to have some sort of structure, so that roles and situations are made available to children. This does not necessarily mean that roles have to be decided upon and allocated to children, but materials have to be provided that allow particular kinds of roles to be taken on.

Play in a multi-ethnic context

There are many important subliminal messages in the structuring of play. If, for example, the home corner contains only Western-style saucepans and crockery, then this carries the message that this is the only proper way in which food can be prepared and served. Children from other cultural backgrounds thus have their own homes and culture devalued, and children from a Western cultural background will unwittingly have the idea reinforced that theirs is the only way of

organising things. Home corners need to be equipped with chapati pans and woks in the kitchen, saris and lunghis in the dressing-up box and dolls of three or four different racial appearances (facially, and not just skin colour).

Play and gender roles

It is also important to try to avoid gender stereotyping in play. There are three major ways in which you can actively ensure that equal opportunities are encouraged.

• Use non-specific language when describing jobs; for example, use fire-fighter rather than fireman, police officer rather than policeman or -woman, refuse collectors rather than dustmen, and so on. Most jobs that have gender-specific names have equally good names that are not specific, contrived or clumsy.

• Suggest roles to boys and to girls that reverse stereotypes.

The example of male nurses and female doctors has been used in classrooms for many years. However, many girls still see the kitchen in the home corner as their domain and many boys still expect to have the commanding roles. Simply suggesting that 'Brian wash up now, because Brenda's going off to work' will help counter this.

• When the question of gender roles is raised, be specific about equal opportunity issues. If children protest that nursing/cleaning up/changing nappies is girls' work, then *they* have stopped the role-play, and it's quite appropriate to have a short discussion about gender stereotypes.

CONTEXTS

Structuring contexts for play

Home corners need not necessarily be homes. It is possible, with minimal equipment or items that are easy to collect, to transform them into a whole variety of different places, each of which will offer a series of new roles to take on and explore. Any context will need to reflect aspects of some of the children's experiences, but these experiences need not necessarily be first-hand. Children are aware of a very wide range of environments and places, particularly through television, and will use these experiences very naturally in their play. This provides scope for the home corner to reflect the contemporary curriculum that you have planned for your class and the children's recent collective experiences.

As children develop in the primary school, teachers tend to move towards more structured forms of play. They introduce role-play and drama in which locations and characters are described (with various degrees of looseness), and the children use their experience and knowledge of the situation, coupled with their everyday social knowledge, to explore the motivations and emotions of other people.

Just as with play in the home corner, the teacher needs to decide how much structure is needed and what are the most appropriate ways in which to provide it. For example, setting out a table under a sign saying 'post office', with some postage stamps, scales, envelopes and rubber stamps, may offer sufficient context for nursery and reception aged children to 'write' letters, post, sort and deliver them. However, although older children may need fewer physical accoutrements, they will probably need more defined roles – the office worker in a hurry to post a letter, stuck in the queue behind the

I want those!

pensioner with a mislaid pension book, the harassed desk clerk, and so on.

The contexts which follow are basic suggestions for locations for play and role-play. Each assumes that the children are fairly familiar with the environment, directly or indirectly.

Shops

Supermarket

Provide lots of empty packets, a till, some shopping bags and a few signs. Play can be extended to include deliveries, food packaging and restocking. Having as many packets of the same product as possible makes the setting more realistic.

Try some of the following role-play situations.

• What happens when the stocks of one type of grocery run out? What do the shop assistants and managers do? Whom do they contact? How much new stock should they reorder and how do they pay for it?

• A customer comes back to complain about some food that he bought which was off, and blames the shop. What does the manager say in reply? What does she do if the customer comes back the next day with a similar complaint? What do the other customers think?

Shoe shop

Provide old shoes, boots, a chair or two, and perhaps a foot gauge (home-made or borrowed from a local store). Children might be given the roles of different kinds of customer, with particular needs.

• A mother and child are buying shoes for the child. The mother wants a 'sensible' shoe, but the child wants something stylish which costs twice as much. How does the shop assistant make a sale?

• Meanwhile, a long queue of would-be customers has formed and they are getting impatient. What are their comments about the situation?

Clothes shop

Lots of dressing-up clothes, a hanger rail and a cheval mirror give the bare bones for this type of shop, though you can add tills, changing rooms, price tags and security devices if you wish. This provides a good and familiar location for different roles, and gives scope for incidents to occur. Try the following role-play situations.

• A customer, while browsing, slips a pair of socks into his own bag instead of the store's basket. What happens when the store detective challenges the customer? The customer insists that he was going to pay for the goods at the checkout. What happens then?
• A customer complains to the manager, insisting that a sweater bought at the store the week before shrank when she washed it even though she followed the instructions on the label.

Post office
A post office provides a wonderful location for early writing, with lots of forms to fill in. (Help yourself to a selection from your local post office.) Younger children will write, stick stamps and sell goods. Rubber stamps and ink pads are very popular for franking, and some weighing of parcels can take place. Older children might get into the problems of sorting and delivery. Try the following role-play situations.
• Wrap up and address lots of different objects. Customers can then take them to the post office where the staff weigh them and calculate the postage cost using a rate table.
• Address a couple of hundred small envelopes (wage-packet size) to different places in the UK. How fast can the post office sort them for delivery? What is the most efficient way to do the sorting?

Transport

Buses
A conductor's hat is easier to get hold of than a ticket machine, although you could use the old-fashioned preprinted kind of ticket. Set up chairs in rows, fill up the seats, and no more standing in the aisle...!
   Try the following role-play situations.
• The bus is full and lots of people are standing. Two

people get off at the next stop, but the conductor won't let any of those queuing at the bus stop get on to the bus. What do these people do and say?

• The sign on the front of the bus says it is going to Elm Street, but this is a mistake as the bus is really scheduled to go only as far as Oak Avenue. What happens when the bus stops at Oak Avenue and a lot of the passengers want to go on a further two miles? How do the driver and conductor explain the situation?

Stations

Lots of things can go on here: there are tickets to buy and trains to miss, buffets about to close down and the bookshop. You could also add transport police, porters, a few passengers and some unintelligible loudspeaker announcements!

Try the following role-play situations.

• There is a long queue of people who are trying to leave the station having just completed a long and delayed train journey. The ticket collector is insisting on meticulously checking all the tickets. Two people at the end of the queue are in a desperate

hurry and keep trying to push their way forward....

• There are two platforms at the station. A group of people are waiting for a train to North Town on Platform One, when they hear a partly inaudible announcement which mentions North Town and Platform Two. What happens? Who moves? There is no guard or station attendant around to ask. When the train arrives what do the people on the wrong platform say and do?

Trains

Arrange chairs as if they were seats on the train, and have ticket inspectors, buffet car attendants and dining cars – or make it a commuter train and have none of these, not even enough seats for everyone! *Now* is the chance for children to discover what happens if they pull the emergency communication chain! You

could also try the following role-play situations.
• All the second class seats are taken and an elderly couple decide to sit in the empty first-class compartment rather than stand for the long journey. But when the ticket collector arrives he is not very happy about this. What happens?
• A passenger has bought a bacon sandwich in the buffet car. It is delicious, and she's half-way through eating it when a British Rail inspector insists that it is not an official British Rail sandwich, but one that the steward has dishonestly made from his own supplies, pocketing the money for himself. The inspector wants the remains of the

sandwich as evidence, the passenger wants to finish it, and the buffet steward insists that he's innocent!

Airports
This context provides even more elaborate tickets to check, tear out, punch and so on, plus boarding cards, passports, customs and shops. There's lots of scope for a whole series of mini-encounters as children move through the terminal to the aircraft.
  Try the following role-play situations.
• Security checks on passengers travelling by plane might involve luggage searches, questioning, X-ray machines, passport checks and so on. How can this be done so that people are not held up for too long?
• When leaving an airport everyone walks through the

green channel at customs, but how do the customs officers spot who is carrying contraband and excess goods?

Health services

Surgery
In this context you can set up waiting rooms, receptionists, nurses and doctors – plus the notices, forms and packets of records.
  Try the following role-play situations.
• There is a long queue in the surgery waiting room and someone has been in with the doctor for a long time. The doctor comes to the door and says she has got an emergency case and could everyone not requiring urgent attention please come back on another day. She returns to her patient, but nobody in the waiting room moves....
• Brief lots of patients with different needs such as some to see the nurse, people needing repeat prescriptions, holiday vaccination enquiries, physiotherapy and

appointments with the doctor. Once they are all briefed let them all loose on the two receptionists and the secretary!

Hospital
Some children will have had direct experience of hospital, but they will all have seen something about hospitals on television. There are an enormous number of potential roles and situations to create, or you could simply provide a little play equipment, a couple of improvised beds and a uniform or two, and let the children take over from there. Alternatively, you could try a role-play situation where every bed is filled with a patient

awaiting surgery. The nurses start the pre-operation routines, when there's an emergency admission, an acute case needing a bed immediately. What happens?

Veterinary surgeon
This works best after a visit to a real veterinary surgery. Set up the surgery with waiting rooms, baskets, toy pets, receptionists and so on. This might usefully be linked to a classroom pet shop.
　　Try the following role-play situations.
• The vet's receptionist mistakenly mixes up the pet medicines for two pets. Soon after the owners have left with their pets, the vet and the receptionist discover the error.
• In the waiting room, one owner's pet eats another owner's pet....

Optician
Again, this context works best after a visit to a real optician. Collect old spectacles (frames only are safest), and make up eye charts for testing. Again, there are forms to fill in and lots of questions to be asked and answered.
　　Try the following role-play situations.
• A customer just can't make up his mind about the style of frames he prefers. Various assistants and his family offer him advice to help him make up his mind.
• There is a queue of customers waiting to collect their new glasses and the assistant who is carrying them in from the storeroom drops the case, mixing them all up.

Workplaces

Bakery
Visit the local bakers and then set up your own – preferably making and baking real dough. Interview the workers to see

what goes on and ask customers what they want. This situation can supply a chance to write recipe books, find out health and safety regulations, dress up – and provide something to eat at the end!

Try the following role-play situations.
• The delivery of flour for the night's baking hasn't arrived. What can the bakery manager and her staff do?
• The bakery manager asks the early morning shift to bake an extra dozen batches. He doesn't mention any extra bonus or overtime payment. What do the workers say?

Café
Two locations are needed for this – the dining area and the kitchens backstage. Provide a few dressing-up clothes for the staff and some menus and cutlery. There's also scope for maths work in this, working out bills and estimating quantities.

Try the following role-play situations.
• A customer complains, quite unreasonably, about the service. The manager insists that the customer is always right, but the waitress disagrees.
• The café staff hear that a public health inspector will be arriving in the afternoon. The staff know that the manager has been rather lax. If the inspector finds out he might decide to close the café and they will lose their jobs. What do they do?

Building site
Visit a site and then start planning some buildings. The children can plan and lay out building bricks, discuss the needs of the people who will use their building, and organise who does what among all the trades that are found in the construction industry.

Try the following role-play situations.
• For a dare, a building site worker 'borrows' a small piece of machinery to show his friends in the pub that evening. The security guard notices him taking it off the site and accuses him of stealing. The site manager is all set to sack him, despite the worker's assertions that he was going to bring the machinery back the next morning. What happens next?
• The bricklayers are taking longer over their work than was expected. Therefore, the carpenters, electricians and plasterers have nothing to do. The manager wants to lay them off until the brickwork is ready, but they are not happy with this idea. Some of them are saying that the bricklayers are dragging the job out so that they earn more money....

CHAPTER 10

Imaginary worlds

Role-play can be extended and structured to make a long-running series of activities that develop sophisticated discussion and other oral skills as the situation develops and becomes more complex. This chapter describes some scenarios in which this might happen and, more importantly, shows some of the incidents which the teacher might put before the children as part of each session.

Staying in role over a period of several weeks allows for the emergence of substantial characterisation.

Extending the activity for such a period also allows you to interact with the situation that the children have created themselves. The incident or task which you give them at the beginning of each new session can be a response to the previous session's conclusion.

BACKGROUND

The example around which this chapter is based is drawn from the social studies area of the curriculum. I use the term 'social studies' as a form of shorthand, to refer to all those subjects and cross-curricular themes in the National Curriculum that include references to how people behave socially. These include history, much of geography, the cross-curricular themes of economic and industrial understanding and citizenship, aspects of environmental education, technology and some parts of science.

Social studies uses our experiences of our own contemporary society as a basis for comparison with other social groups, different from ours in time or place (or both). So when a child learns about how another social group does something – such as how people build homes in South-east Asia or how families lived and worked in Britain in the Middle Ages – she is at the same time comparing and contrasting these accounts with what she already knows about how such matters are conducted in her own society. There is a spiral process going on, where new information about social activities is used to test and then confirm,

update or amend hypotheses about the way people live and work in social groups.

This kind of social learning is very much based on speaking and listening to others. Meanings of words and ideas are shared through dialogue, and social meanings in particular are mediated through speech.

Social concepts

It is possible to suggest a set of essential social concepts, such as those in the check-list below, that help us explain how societies are organised. Such concepts are not intended to be 'taught' to children in a dogmatic or didactic manner, but they can be used as a check-list to help children express their own analyses, in

their own words, of examples of similar experiences. Ultimately, children may come to use, for example, the expression 'the division of labour', but in the meantime the phrase 'sharing out the jobs' may be perfectly adequate for their needs. Concepts are not simply acquired in an all-or-none fashion, but slowly developed, shared and refined. It is meaningless to say, for example, that a child has 'grasped' the concept of power. Power is a multi-faceted concept and a six-year-old may see relationships of power in terms of adults and children, police and public, monarchs and subjects, while an eleven-year-old may have a more

sophisticated concept of power, including elections, premiers and presidents, hierarchical relationships at work, historical contexts and so on.

The following check-list of social studies concepts is loosely based on that in the ILEA handbook *Social Studies in the Primary School* (ILEA, 1980).

The distribution of power and authority

Power is the ability to do as you wish and to make others do as you want them to. Authority is based on the respect and obedience that is given to someone, either because of some official position that they hold, or because it is felt that they have great personal abilities or qualities. In most social groups, power is exercised by

an individual or group and is distributed unequally. Power and authority can often be held by the same people, but you can have power without authority (an armed bank robber) or authority without power (an unarmed police officer).

The division of labour

The division of labour is a term used to describe the dividing of work into a number of separate parts, each of which is undertaken by a different individual or group. This division may be decided on for the sake of efficiency (it gets the task completed more quickly and cheaply), it may be based on custom and tradition ('a woman's place...'), or it may be the result of the distribution of power. The division of labour may lead to a feeling of alienation from work because, for example, the contribution made by one individual seems a very small part of the end product.

Tradition

All societies and groups have traditions, or customary ways of doing things, passed on from generation to generation. Ideas and habits established in this way can be expressed through simple everyday events, through celebrations among families and friends, to festivals shared by a wider community.

Social change

Societies and groups change in the way that they behave. Social change can happen for political, economic or technological reasons, among others, and may happen at different rates among different groups.

Social control

All groups and societies exercise social control over the behaviour of their members by making and enforcing rules and laws, and by expecting members to behave according to particular conventions. These sorts of constraints range from formal laws, written and agreed by parliament, through the unwritten laws of playground games, to the conventions of 'please' and 'thank you'. Sanctions are imposed on those individuals and groups who break the rules or laws. When conventions are flouted there may not be punishment, but there will almost certainly be disapproval.

Conflict

In all societies some resources will be limited and there will be competition and conflict about the distribution of these resources. Conflict also occurs about the aims and values of a society. Children are aware of conflict around them and they need to understand that it is an inevitable and necessary part of society, and that there are various ways by which conflict is limited and resolved. Conflicts are often related to the division of labour and of power.

Interdependence

People in social groups depend on each other in a variety of ways. This interdependence can range from reciprocal caring and emotional support to the exchange of goods and services. Interdependence can occur at the level of individuals and all the way up to the international level.

Co-operation

People in social groups often agree to work and organise together in order to lighten common tasks and solve common problems. This may well involve the need to compromise individual needs and wants. Through co-operation, groups may be able to perform tasks which cannot be done by individuals working alone.

CONTEXTS

Contexts for role-play

Extended role-play, inventing and organising an imaginary world, can help develop social concepts and ideas through talk. The suggestions that follow indicate several basic scenarios and offer a series of possible activities or situations which should be selected and adapted to suit your aims for the children. The whole class could work as a single group, but the ideas will probably work better with small groups of about six to eight. It is possible to allow the groups to interact at various points, if this seems useful. After each session of role-play, it may be useful to draw the whole class together to compare some of the points that have arisen. The children will be able to contrast different ways of tackling a problem, and it may often be possible to draw out points from the discussion and use them in role-play. You may be able to link the children's behaviour in the role-play to some contemporary social issue, or make some historical or cross-cultural comparison.

Setting the basic scene

Ask the children to create their own society. There are several possible ways of doing this; role-playing a group of travellers shipwrecked on a desert island or marooned in space are two popular possibilities. The important elements are:
• isolation from adults and adult help;
• scarcity of some kind of resources;
• relatively simple and manageable technology;
• a series of 'natural' pressures that require the children to attempt to co-operate.

Establish the initial role-play so that the children are firmly in role – for example, they could board ship for a holiday cruise. They will have to sort out their cabin allocations, write letters home, organise deck games, practise lifeboat drills and so on. Use the latter activity to divide the children naturally into the groups you wish to use later. Only when a routine has been established will you need to let them know that, for example, a storm has

blown up and the ship is in danger. Send the children to the lifeboats, without any of their imaginary belongings, or alternatively you could give the group just enough time to select one thing to be taken on the lifeboat.

Each group can then be shipwrecked on a different small island. This means that each group can remain as a separate self-contained society, at least for the time being, and it allows you plausibly to have different activities for each group, if you so wish.

The first activity you organise must be for the children to explore their islands. You could provide an outline map for them to fill in or you could give them a list of resources that they must locate. The essential part of the activity is for them to define the physical limits of their island and discover the major resources, such as fresh water, wild animals, woods, fruit-bearing plants, vegetables and fish. They will also need to

find out any potentially dangerous aspects – fierce animals, high or steep cliffs and mountains, sharks and so on. As well as mapping their island, each group might usefully make a model of it. The map and the model will form a useful constraint on future activities, as a reminder of the limitations of the island.

Probably the next activity would be to ask the groups to decide where they want to establish their bases. They will need very little direction from you in this, and they should be allowed to decide their own priorities and make their own decisions. If they place themselves in a situation that you consider ill-advised (for example, at a great distance from fresh water), then you can give them a task at the next session that will stress the disadvantages of their site. For example, you could say, 'It is getting to be midday, and the

temperature is going up and up. You have no drinking water left. What do you do?' You should then let them decide whether or not to move camp.

After these initial activities, which will probably need to occur in the order suggested, the next set of incidents can be ordered by you to match the needs and progress of each group. Each activity is designed to develop one or more of the concepts outlined on pages 153 to 154.

Developmental activities

Priorities
What do the children need? What do they want? Ask each group to draw up a list of all the things that they'd like to

do, now they are free of parental and school control on their island. Then remind them that their time, resources and energy are limited. Get them to discuss and agree how to divide their list into things that are absolute necessities, things that they feel that they need, but might be able to get away without, and the extra luxuries. To which will they give priority? Why are these more important?

After the role-play, discuss how priorities are made in real life. How do people in families, schools, workplaces and the country as a whole decide what will be tackled as a priority? This discussion will introduce the concepts of *co-operation* and *conflict*.

Jobs to be done

Who will do which jobs? There's lots to be done to keep alive on the island, even if the group concentrate only on their list of most essential needs. Ask the groups to break down their needs into lists of tasks to be done, and to allocate the jobs between them.

How will they do this? Can they arrange it so that people use their individual skills, or is it just assumed that, for example, the boys are stronger or the girls are better at cooking? Are the tasks distributed so that one person (perhaps a child taking a dominant part in the discussion) receives a lighter load than the others? Is some sort of rota established to spread the tasks evenly?

Don't stop the children planning whatever they choose, but note their

decisions and then tell them it is now a week later, and offer them some appropriate information. For example, if they choose a rota, point out that it seemed, for example, that the two children who collected firewood on Tuesday took twice as long as everyone else and the wood was damp, while Wednesday's cook burned all the food, and so on. Ask them what the point of sharing out the jobs fairly is, if some of them don't get done properly. Can they afford fairness when their lives are at stake? If they chose to specialise, ask them if it's fair that two children can disappear 'hunting' all day, and come back to find all the cooking and cleaning done?

Your objective is to indirectly challenge the children's choices and to make them see the various problems that can arise from their decisions.

After the role-play, discuss with the class the different solutions and problems that were encountered. Is there a

fair way of allocating jobs? The talk will touch on the concepts of the *distribution of power and authority*, the *division of labour*, *co-operation* and *interdependence*.

Who's in charge?

Some groups may emerge with the idea of having a leader, a person entrusted to make decisions. Ask the groups to decide if they want a leader and if so, what will this child's tasks be and how will she be selected? This may lead to some dissent within the group, as would-be leaders find that they have no followers and others find that they have to

choose between two candidates. How *do* they choose? Some groups may well decide not to have a leader, but to share the decision-making instead.

Whatever is decided, your role is to offer a variation on their chosen situation that challenges the children's concept of leadership. If a dominant child has assumed the leadership and the others tacitly accepted this, you could brief another child to challenge a questionable decision, and to attempt to gain the support of the others. If the children always discuss each issue, create a situation where an immediate response is needed in the face of some danger. If a leader is elected, brief a child

to challenge the process as being time-wasting and not leading to sensible and firm decisions.

After the role-play, discuss whether 'strong' leaders are needed in their societies or in larger social groups such as countries. The relationship of prime minister and monarch usually fascinates children. This raises the concepts of the *distribution of power and authority*, and *conflict*.

Laying down the law

Does the island society need laws or rules? Brief one child to announce that he will not do his agreed share of the work, because the others can't make him. How do the other children react? If they accept the situation, point out that this means extra work for all of them. If they try to insist that

he rejoins the group, ask them what authority they have to do this.

Ask the group to decide if they need rules to govern what people should do. If so, how should the rules be made and what should the rules be? (These three stages may tend to run together: it can lead to more interesting discussions if they are kept as separate stages, but this may not be easy.) Again, present the children with situations that make them critically analyse their decision-making process and the decisions they came to. For example, if one child simply made up all the rules, brief some of the others to challenge this. If a rule is framed very ambiguously, brief a child to interpret it in a way that wasn't intended, and to defend herself on the grounds that what she did was permitted.

After the role-play, discuss how rules and laws are made. What rules does the school have? Why? How are the country's rules decided? What happens if rules are sloppily drawn up? Who should make the rules and how? What sort of areas should the rules cover?

One group of children I worked with once made a rule that no-one should undertake dangerous activities, because if they hurt themselves more work would be created for the rest of the group. This led to a discussion on whether laws should interfere with people's liberties. For example, should people be forbidden to smoke?

Such discussions involve concepts of *social control*.

The law in action

What happens if a rule or law is broken? Assuming that the children have created a rule that no one shall steal, the following scenario could be attempted. If other rules have been made, variations can be devised that challenge these.

Brief one child that he wakes in the night and sees a shadowy figure leaving the food store. This figure looks rather like another member of the group. Brief this other child that she slept all through the night and then tell the

whole group that in the
morning they find some food
has gone missing from the
store.

What happens? Usually, the
first child accuses the other or
at least reports what he saw.
How do the children sort out
whether the accusation is true
or not? Is the accusation,
coupled with the fact of the
'crime' enough evidence? Who
will decide? Will the accused
be able to offer a defence?

After the role-play, discuss
how the law is enforced: the
distinctions between the
police, who investigate and

apprehend suspects; the
prosecution service, who make
accusations in court; and the
courts, which hear evidence
and make decisions about
innocence and guilt. Do the
children need all of these
processes? How can their trials
be fair? Do real-life trials
always end up with a fair
result?

You could move on to
discuss what happens to those
found guilty of wrong-doing.
Can the island society afford to
have a prison? One person
locked up and another to guard
her means two fewer pairs of
hands to work. Will prison
make the child less likely to
offend in future? This draws
upon concepts of the
*distribution of power and
authority*, and *social control*.

Coming to a decision

How are major decisions
arrived at? Put it to the
children that they could spend
some time preparing a boat to
leave the island. Do they want
to do this or would they rather
stay on the island? Try to get
the group to split over this.
Emphasise to the 'stay-on-the-
island' group the delights of a
parent-free, school-free
existence and stress the lack of
home comforts, television and
friends to the 'go-home' group.

This is a major decision: the
go-home group needs everyone
to work on boat-building if
they are to have any hope of
succeeding. There has to be a
decision, but how will they
decide? How do the losers and
winners feel about it? Do the
losers accept the decision, and
if it is decided to build a boat,
will they join in? If it is
decided to stay on the island,
will the would-be boat builders
abandon their plans?

After the role-play, discuss the idea of majority decisions taking effect. Is this fair? Are there dangers in overlooking the rights and needs of minorities? How can they be protected? This involves concepts of the *division of labour*, *conflict* and *co-operation*.

Anniversaries and memories

It is exactly a year after the children arrived on the island. What will they do? Will they celebrate and if so, how? Then imagine it's two years after the landing.

After the role-play, discuss how and why people celebrate anniversaries and festivals.

This introduces the concepts of *tradition* and *social change*.

A fair exchange?

Set up a situation in which some children can produce something better than others. Allow them to specialise in their work, and ask how they are going to use the extra things they make. Will they give them away, sell them or store them? Encourage the children to swap and exchange the things they make. How do they decide what is a fair exchange?

You could involve two different island groups in this, with each island specialising in one commodity. This could lead to some trade between the two and you can explore with them the idea of exchange rates and how these are fixed. You could ask the children to

explore also what happens when there is a surplus of the major commodity on one island and a fall in production of the other's principal export. What does this do to the exchange rate? You could bring in a third island, that can very easily undercut one of the other two islands' prices. What might happen then?

After the role-play, the enormous area of trade and exchange could be discussed, including relationships between developed and developing nations. The discussion will probably involve the concepts of the *division of labour*, *social change*, *conflict* and i*nterdependence*.

An end to it all

Once you have completed a sequence of activities, find some suitable way to end the role-play. Perhaps the islands are discovered by a rescue party or perhaps the children do eventually build a boat and escape.

CHAPTER 11

Recording and assessing

The preceding chapters of this book have stressed the importance of continuously evaluating children's listening and talking skills. Evaluation is an essential component of planning effective learning. Assessment can be rather different. If tests of competence are established, without reference to the specific needs of particular children, then it is almost inevitable that these tests will dominate and determine the direction of the educational processes, with teachers 'teaching to the test'. Assessment inevitably affects the curriculum that children are offered, so it becomes vital that the assessment is designed to measure the underlying intentions of the curriculum, rather than superficial evidence that is easy to collect.

There is a particular problem with speaking and listening. Because talk is about something, it becomes all too easy to confuse talk as an accomplishment (the skills of talking) with talk as a medium (what the talk is about). What interests us in this context is how well children are able to talk and listen – in what contexts and with what sense of audience – rather than whether they have a vast knowledge of a particular subject or whether they are logical.

Gathering data

What you decide to evaluate will vary according to the children's age, the context and the activity. Generally, it would seem useful to observe each child's talking and listening patterns as he or she works with:
• the teacher;
• other children in a small group;
• other children in a large group.

Most observations will take place within the context of classroom activities, but there may be occasions when it is noted that a child operates in a different way in out-of-class contexts, perhaps with more fluency. This is worth noting and recording; it will be useful to consider why such a change is apparent and whether and how that fluency might be brought into classroom use.

Most observations will be made on the spot in the classroom. Occasionally, you may wish to make a recording (tape or video) of an activity, in order to analyse it at comparative leisure. There are some suggestions concerning how to go about this in Chapter 12.

Evaluating and assessing developmental strands

As is described in greater detail in the National Curriculum guide (see pages 171 and 172), the various attainment targets can be linked together into developmental strands. These strands represent different aspects or skills of talking and listening that have been identified from the National Curriculum English document. There are seven of these as can be seen in the diagram below.

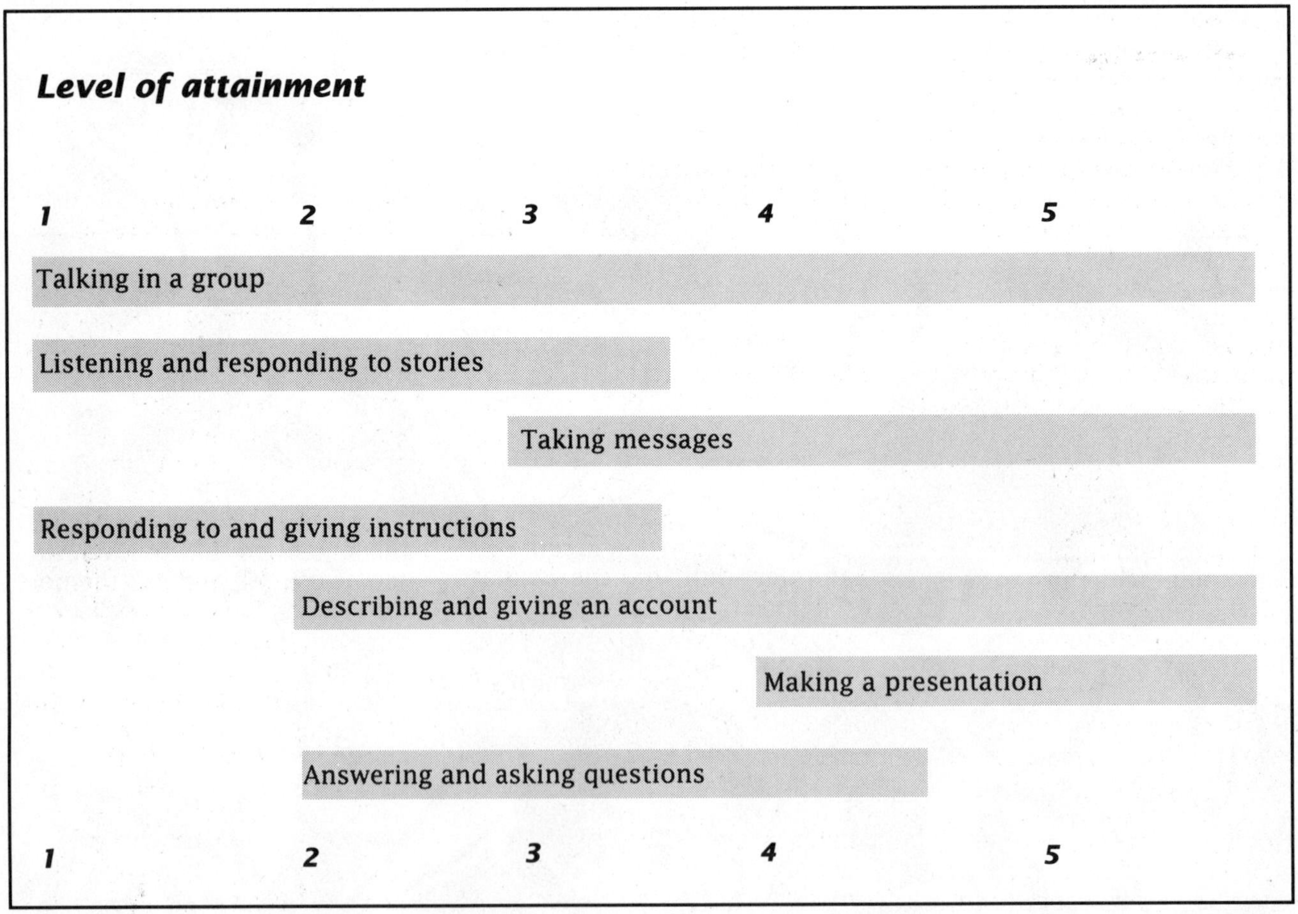

Level of attainment

1	2	3	4	5

Talking in a group

Listening and responding to stories

Taking messages

Responding to and giving instructions

Describing and giving an account

Making a presentation

Answering and asking questions

1	2	3	4	5

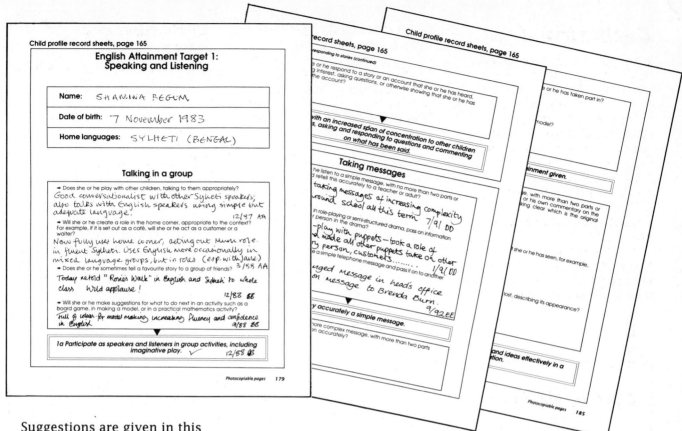

The image above contains the following handwritten record sheets:

Child profile record sheets, page 165

English Attainment Target 1:
Speaking and Listening

Name: SHAMINA BEGUM

Date of birth: 7 November 1983

Home languages: SYLHETI (BENGAL)

Talking in a group

➤ Does she or he play with other children, talking to them appropriately?

Good conversationalist with other Sylheti speakers; also talks with English speakers using simple but adequate language. 12/87 AA

➤ Will she or he create a role in the home corner, appropriate to the context? For example, if it is set out as a café, will she or he act as a customer or a waiter?

Now fully uses home corner, acting out Mum role in fluent Sylheti. Uses English more occasionally in mixed language groups, but in roles (esp. with Jane). 3/58 AA

➤ Does she or he sometimes tell a favourite story to a group of friends?

Today retold "Rosie's Walk" in English and Sylheti to whole class   Wild applause!   12/88 BB

➤ Will she or he make suggestions for what to do next in an activity such as a board game, in making a model, or in a practical mathematics activity?

Full of ideas for model making, increasing fluency and confidence in English   9/88 BB

1a Participate as speakers and listeners in group activities, including imaginative play. ✓   12/58 BB

Photocopiable pages   179

---

responding to stories (continued)

...she or he respond to a story or an account that she or he has heard, ...g interest, asking questions, or otherwise showing that she or he has ...the account?

...with an increased span of concentration to other children ...s, asking and responding to questions and commenting on what has been said.

Taking messages

...he listen to a simple message, with no more than two parts or ...d retell this accurately to a teacher or adult?

...taking messages of increasing complexity around school all this term 7/91 DD

...in role-playing or semi-structured drama, pass on information ...r person in the drama?

...play with puppets—took a role of ...d made all other puppets take on other ...y person, customers......... 1/91 DD

...e a simple telephone message and pass it on to another

...nged message in head's office ...on message to Brenda Burn   9/92 EE

...y accurately a simple message.

...more complex message, with more than two parts ...on accurately?

Photocopiable pages   185

...she or he has taken part in?

...model?

...inment given.

...e, with more than two parts ...or his own commentary on the ...king clear which is the original

...she or he has seen, for example.

...lost, describing its appearance?

...and ideas effectively in a ...tion.

Suggestions are given in this chapter for ways to evaluate a child's attainment in relation to each strand. Photocopiable pages 179 to 191 provide a record which can be used to mark and date each child's approximate progress along each strand. Taking all of the strands together, it is possible to make an estimate of the overall 'level of attainment' for a child in speaking and listening. But the record will be more useful in formative assessment if the progress along each strand is considered separately. If a child has, for example, successfully reached Level 3 in describing and giving an account, then the next set of activities for that child will need to be selected to move him towards Level 4 – in this case, helping him to give more detailed accounts and to offer a variety of explanations for something happening. The attainment target charts on pages 173 and 174 are arranged to help you select appropriate activities to bring about this progression.

In the case of children who are emerging bilingual speakers, it will be important to note, where possible, their development in both their home language and English. This would usefully be done in consultation with a parent or another adult who speaks that language, or by observing two children interacting who share the same language.

It is important to recognise that a child may have a sophisticated set of oral skills in her home language, but have a far less developed set of skills in English. The child's acquisition of the same degree of skill in English will be enhanced by developing skills in the home language alongside work in oral English.

Evaluating progress along each strand of development

In each strand, the statements of attainment are given in italics and between the statements a number of questions are posed. If you can answer each of these positively for a child, then move on past the statement that follows, to the next level, and ask the next set of questions of the child. The questions that are asked may indicate a particular context, for example, a science activity, but this is intended to be indicative rather than prescriptive.

This evaluation process need only take place a couple of times a year and need not be done in the classroom with the children present.

CHAPTER 12

Resources and books

There is no particular specialist equipment that is essential to the development of speaking and listening skills for most children. However, those with some special needs will, of course, need particular resources.

But learning can be made more effective, more enjoyable and more extensive if a school can provide each class with some equipment.

The following pages provide some information about useful audio equipment to support speaking and listening. There is also a list of books which are recommended for further reading on the subject, and a selection of useful addresses.

Equipment

Tape recorders

Tape recorders are one of the most useful and versatile tools for speaking and listening. They need not be particularly expensive models – it is better to have two or three simple machines per class than just one elaborate model. However, it will be useful for a school to have at least one tape recorder capable of copying tapes.

The simple tape recorder will ideally have only one record button (rather than the variety which has two buttons to be pressed simultaneously, which many young children find difficult). Headsets,

particularly if used with a junction box that allows several children to listen at the same time, can be very helpful in getting group activities going quietly.

A dubbing tape recorder will be particularly useful for making copies of tapes, particularly tapes of stories. English and other community language stories can be recorded from children's favourite books and the tapes can then be used in class alongside the book. It is useful to keep the original recording centrally, and make copies available for class use, so that you don't have to re-record too often. Removing the plastic tag on the back of the cassette (opposite the side that engages with the recorder) will ensure that the tape cannot

accidentally be recorded over or erased. Label all tapes of stories with both the name of the story and the language in which it is recorded.

Making recordings in class can be easier if an area of the classroom is designated as a recording area. This area should preferably be carpeted, with cushions to sit on to minimise background noise. It also helps to reduce background noise if you rest the recorder on a felt mat or something soft, because resting it directly on a table can allow stray noises to be inadvertently recorded.

There are advantages and disadvantages to using tape recorders with internal microphones. An external microphone can be pointed at the direction of the speaker and will thus give clearer recordings, but an internal

microphone of the omni-directional kind will be less obtrusive, and is less likely to malfunction or get lost.

Video-recorders

The use of a video-recorder is becoming increasingly possible in primary schools, as simple small machines become relatively cheaper. Their use in developing speaking and listening skills will vary from activity to activity. A child-made tape of an educational visit might, for example, be an excellent basis for making a series of alternative voice-over narratives.

A major use of the video-recorder in the future may well be to supplant the tape recorder as a way of monitoring children's talk and discussion. It is far easier to view, analyse and if necessary transcribe a video-tape of discussion or dialogue than it is to follow an audio recording. It is much clearer which child makes which interjection, and all the visual contexts and clues of non-verbal behaviour make it simpler to analyse children's meanings, performance and level of skill.

Other audio equipment

Other kinds of equipment have occasionally been referred to in earlier chapters. Two items that will be particularly useful are telephones and radios. Even non-working models in the home corner will stimulate particular kinds of speaking and listening, but children should also have access to real phones.

Further reading

The following books will be of interest to teachers wishing to look more deeply into the development of children's talking and listening skills.

Barnes, D. (1976) *From Communication to Curriculum*, Penguin.

Barrs, M., Ellis, S., Hester, H. and Thomas, A. (1990) *Patterns of Learning: The Primary Language Record and the National Curriculum*, Centre for Language in Primary Education.

Bruner, J. (1984) *Child's Talk: Learning to Use Language*, Oxford University Press.

Corson, D. (1987) *Oral language across the Curriculum*, Multilingual Matters.

Edwards, D. and Mercer, N. (1987) *Common Knowledge: The Development of Understanding in the Classroom*, Methuen.

ILEA (1988) *The Primary Language Record: a handbook for teachers*, ILEA/Centre for Language in Primary Education.

Mathematical Association (1987) *Maths Talk*, Mathematical Association/ Stanley Thornes.

National Oracy Project (journal, from 1989) *TALK: the journal of the National Oracy Project* (about twice a year).

Norman, K. (1990) *Teaching, Talking and Learning in Key Stage One*, NCC/National Oracy Project.

Norman, K. (1991) *Teaching, Talking and Learning in Key Stage Two*, NCC/National Oracy Project.

Open University (1991) *Talk and Learning 5 – 16: an in-service pack on oracy for teachers* (P535), Open University.

Pimm, D. (1987) *Speaking Mathematically: Communication in Mathematics Classrooms*, Routledge.

Rosen, M. (1989) *Did I hear you write?* Deutsch.

Steedman, C. (1983) *The Tidy House*, Virago.

Tizard, B. and Hughes, M. (1984) *Young Children Learning: Talking and Thinking at Home and at School*, Fontana.

Trudgill, P. (1975) *Accent, Dialect and the School*, Edward Arnold.

Wells, G. (1987) *The Meaning Makers*, Hodder & Stoughton.

Addresses

The following organisations and professional associations have a particular interest in children's oracy. They generally offer publications for teachers, and sometimes for classroom use.

- Afro Caribbean Education Resource Centre
Wyville School
Wyville Road
London SW8 2TJ

- Centre for Bilingual Development and Community Languages
c/o Lewisham Education Authority
1 Aitken Road
Catford
London SE6 3BL

- Centre for Language in Primary Education
Teachers' Centre
Webber Row
London SE1 8QW

- Language in the National Curriculum
Department of English Studies
University of Nottingham
University Park
Nottingham NG7 2RD

- National Association for the Teaching of English
Birley School Annexe
Fox Lane Site
Frecheville
Sheffield S12 4WY

- National Curriculum Council
15-17 New Street
York YO1 2RA

- National Oracy Project
c/o National Curriculum Council
15-17 New Street
York YO1 2RA

CHAPTER 13

National Curriculum guide

Speaking and listening are the subject of English Attainment Target 1 in the National Curriculum Orders for England and Wales. This is a significant advance on the traditional view of English as only being concerned with writing and reading. As the Order puts it, children should develop their 'understanding of the spoken word and the capacity to express themselves effectively in a variety of speaking and listening activities, matching style and response to audience and purpose'.

The activities in this book develop this target for primary children, that is, up to Level of Attainment 5. The National Curriculum gives 21 different statements of attainment and these can be divided into six or seven strands of development. The reordered statements of attainment are shown below:

Talking in a group
1a Participate in group activities.
2a Participate in group activities on given task.
3 No statement of attainment given.
4c Take part in group discussion/activity, express view and comment.
5b Contribute/respond in discussion, develop ideas, advocate, justify.

Listening and responding to stories
1b Listen attentively and respond to stories and poems.
2c Listen attentively and talk about stories and poems.
3c Listen with increased concentration to children and adults.
4 No statement of attainment given.

Taking messages
2 No statement of attainment given.

3b Convey accurately a simple message.
4 No statement of attainment given.
5c Use language to convey information and ideas effectively.

Responding to and giving instructions
1c Respond appropriately to simple instructions.
2e Respond to more complex instructions and give simple instructions.
3d Give, receive and follow accurately precise instructions.
4 No statement of attainment given.

Describing and giving an account
1 No statement of attainment given.
2b Describe an event, real or imagined, to teacher or pupil.
3a Relate real or imaginary events in a connected narrative

which conveys meaning.
4a Give a detailed oral account, or explain with reasons.
5a Give a well-organised and sustained account.

Making a presentation
3 No statement of attainment given.
4d Participate in a presentation.
5d Contribute to the planning and giving of a presentation.

Answering and asking questions
1 No statement of attainment given.
2d Talk, listen, ask and answer questions.
3c Ask and respond to questions and comment.
4b Ask and respond to questions with increased confidence.
5 No statement of attainment given.

These strands of development make it easier to plan programmes of activities that will promote children's development. Each strand has been matched against the various activities in the first six chapters of this book in the form of attainment target charts (173 to 174). Each activity that helps develop particular skills is shown together with the approximate range of attainment levels which it covers. Each activity is identified by two numbers: the bold number refers to the chapter and the second is the number of the activity within the chapter.

When you have identified the particular oral skills that you wish to concentrate on, select the appropriate strand of statements. Reading down the page for the columns that represent your children's ability levels, you can identify a range of activities that match your curriculum plans and your children's specific needs.

National Curriculum Subject guide

All areas of the curriculum will use, in some way, skills of speaking and listening. Many teachers will want to develop oral skills in the process of working in other curriculum areas. Therefore, listed below are curriculum areas that are used or identified in different activities in this book, and the oral skills that can be developed through them. For example, if you had planned that your class should undertake a science topic on animal life, you could look at the science section and find

which activities in the book refer to these.

This section lists the nine core and other foundation subjects and the five cross-curricular themes that have been identified by the National Curriculum Council as being necessary parts of the whole curriculum.

The suggestions given about other curriculum areas include only the activities actually referred to in this book. Many of the activities can be easily extended and developed to cover other programmes of study and attainment targets within the National Curriculum: to list them all would double the length of this book!

English

Writing **1**/1, **1**/4-6.
Reading **1**/4.
Language diversity **6**/12.

Mathematics

General problem-solving **1**/1.
Mathematics as a subject **8**.

Science

Senses **2**/4-5.
Visiting a different environment **2**/1, **2**/8.
Sound **2**/6.
Materials **2**/7.
Weather **2**/9.
Evolution **2**/13.
Animal life **4**/3.
Magnetism **4**/9.
Light **4**/12.

History

Historical visits **2**/1.
Local history **2**/14, **6**/8, **7**.
1930s **6**/7, **6**/13.
1940s **2**/14, **6**/13.
1950s **6**/13.
Schooling **6**/8.
History as a subject **7**.

Geography

Geographical visits **2**/1, **2**/8.
Map-making and using **3**/1, **3**/3-4.
Travel **4**/1.

Technology

Planning events **1**/2.
Solving problems **1**/7.
Production lines **3**/2.
General **3**/5, **4**/10-12.

Art

Drawing **3**/6.

Music

Musical identification **2**/6.

Physical education

Playground games **3**/7.
Rules in sport **3**/9.
General **2**/11, **3**/1.

Cross-curricular themes

Economic and industrial understanding
Planning events **1**/2.
Allocating scarce resources **2**/16.
Discussion questions **5**/14.
Surveys about work **5**/13.
General **4**/5, **6**/14.

Health education
Discussion questions **5**/14.

Environmental education
Environmental surveys **6**/12.
Discussion questions **5**/14.

Citizenship
Group activities **1**/10.
Class councils **5**/10.
Surveys of opinions **6**/12.
Discussion questions **5**/14.
General points **2**/16, **2**/17, **6**/15, **10**.

England and Wales

Strands / Levels	Talking in a group	Listening and responding to stories	Taking messages	Responding to and giving instructions	Describing and giving an account	Making a presentation	Answering and asking questions
1	1/5-8, 5/2, 5/4	1/11-12, 4/1-3, 4/9, 4/11		1/1, 3/1, 3/5, 3/7			
2	1/4-8, 1/13, 2/8, 4/3, 4/5, 4/7-8, 5/1-2, 5/4-5, 5/10-12	1/11-12, 4/1-11, 5/1		1/1, 3/1-8	1/2, 1/7, 1/8-9, 1/16, 2/1, 2/4-11, 2/16, 4/1-2, 4/6		2/1, 6/1-4, 6/13-15
3	1/4-8, 1/13, 2/8, 2/12, 3/1-2, 4/3, 4/5, 4/7-8, 5/1-12, 6/9	4/1-12, 5/1	1/1-3, 1/7-9, 1/11-13, 3/1	1/1-2, 3/1-9	1/1, 1/3, 1/7-9, 1/16, 2/1-17, 3/7-9, 4/1-2, 4/6, 4/9-12	1/5-6, 2/2, 2/9, 2/13, 2/15, 2/17	2/3, 2/8, 2/14, 5/12, 6/1-16
4	1/4-8, 1/10, 1/13, 2/8, 2/12, 2/16-17, 3/1-2, 3/7, 4/3, 4/5, 4/7-8, 5/1-13, 6/9	4/1-5, 4/7-8, 4/10-12, 5/1	1/1-3, 1/7-9, 1/13, 3/1	1/1, 3/1-9	1/1, 1/3, 1/7-9, 1/16, 2/1-17, 3/7-9, 4/2, 5/13	1/5-6, 2/2, 2/9, 2/12-13, 2/15, 2/17, 4/4, 4/9, 4/11-12, 5/8-9	2/8, 2/14, 6/1-16
5	1/4-8, 1/10, 2/12, 2/16-17, 3/2, 3/7, 4/3, 4/5, 4/7-8, 5/1-3, 5/5-13, 6/9		1/1-3, 1/7-9, 1/13, 3/1		1/3, 1/16, 2/2-17, 3/7-9, 5/13	1/5-6, 2/2, 2/9, 2/12-13, 2/15, 2/17, 4/4, 4/9, 4/11-12, 5/8, 5/9	6/5-6, 6/8-16

Scotland

The strand **Audience awareness** is covered in every activity in this book and therefore is not included in this chart.

Chapters 7 to 12 are not organised into activities, but the ideas suggested in them are in the spirit of the Scottish document, *English Language 5-14*.

Strands / Levels	Talking/ listening about information, instructions	Talking/ listening in groups	Talking about experiences, feelings and opinions	Listening awareness of genre	Talking/ listening knowledge about language
A	1/-2, 2/9-10, 2/16, 3/1, 3/5, 3/7	1/5-7, 1/11, 2/4-6, 2/16, 4/2-3, 5/1-6, 5/10-12, 6/1-4	2/4-10, 2/16	4/1-5	
B	1/1-3, 2/9-10, 2/13, 2/16, 3/1-8	1/5-9, 1/11-15, 2/3-6, 2/13, 2/16, 3/1-3, 3/8, 4/2-12, 5/1-12, 6/1-9	2/1-13, 2/16	1/4, 4/1-12	1/11-14, 1/16
C	1/1-3, 2/9-10, 2/13-17, 3/1-9, 6/11-13	1/5-10, 1/13, 1/15, 2/3-6, 2/13-17, 3/1-3, 3/8-9, 4/2-12, 5/1-13, 6/1-17	2/1-17, 6/7-10, 6/12-17	1/4, 4/1-12	1/11-13, 1/16, 3/1-9, 5/1-12
D	1/1-3, 2/9-10, 2/13-17, 3/1-9, 6/11-13	1/5-10, 1/13, 1/15, 2/3-6, 2/13-17, 3/1-3, 3/8-9, 4/2-12, 5/1-13, 6/1-17	2/1-17, 6/7-10, 6/12-17	1/4, 4/2-12	1/13, 1/16, 5/4-12
E	1/1-3, 2/9-10, 2/13-17, 3/3-9, 6/11-13	1/5-10, 2/3-6, 2/13-17, 3/3, 3/8-9, 4/3-12, 5/2-13, 6/1-17	2/1-17, 6/7-10, 6/12-17	1/4, 4/2-12	5/6-13

The pages in this section can be photocopied and adapted to suit your own needs and those of your class; they do not need to be declared in respect of any photocopying licence.

The first three photocopiable pages relate to specific activities in the main body of the book and the appropriate page references are given above each photocopiable sheet.

The assessment sheets provided on pages 179 to 191 form an easy to use record which can be completed for each child and compiled into a booklet to show their individual levels of attainment.

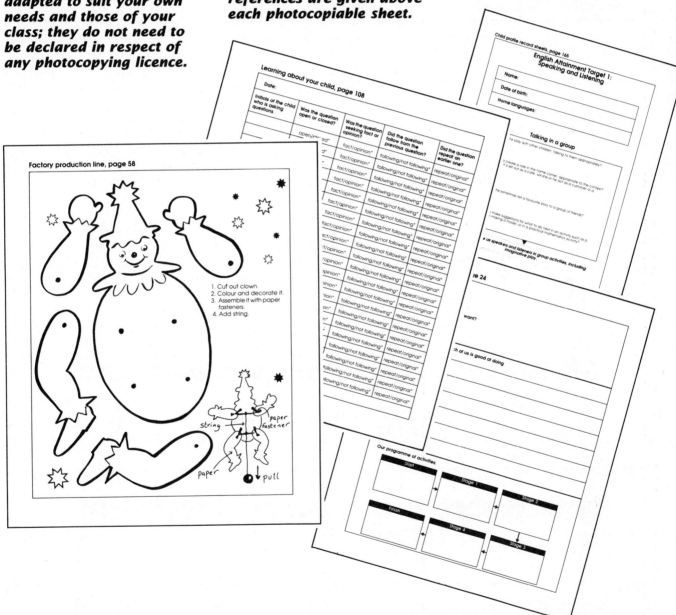

Factory production line, page 58

1. Cut out clown.
2. Colour and decorate it.
3. Assemble it with paper fasteners.
4. Add string.

Learning about your child, page 108

Child profile record sheets, page 165
English Attainment Target 1:
Speaking and Listening

Planning events, page 24

Objective:

Who is it for?

What do they say they want?

Date to be ready by:

Members or group	What each of us is good at doing

Our programme of activities:

Start	Stage 1	Stage 2

Finish	Stage 4	Stage 3

1. Cut out clown.
2. Colour and decorate it.
3. Assemble it with paper fasteners.
4. Add string.

string

paper fastener

paper

pull

Learning about your child, page 108

Date:				
Initials of the child who is asking questions	**Was the question open or closed?**	**Was the question seeking fact or opinion?**	**Did the question follow from the previous question?**	**Did the question repeat an earlier one?**
	open/closed*	fact/opinion*	following/not following*	repeat/original*
	open/closed*	fact/opinion*	following/not following*	repeat/original*
	open/closed*	fact/opinion*	following/not following*	repeat/original*
	open/closed*	fact/opinion*	following/not following*	repeat/original*
	open/closed*	fact/opinion*	following/not following*	repeat/original*
	open/closed*	fact/opinion*	following/not following*	repeat/original*
	open/closed*	fact/opinion*	following/not following*	repeat/original*
	open/closed*	fact/opinion*	following/not following*	repeat/original*
	open/closed*	fact/opinion*	following/not following*	repeat/original*
	open/closed*	fact/opinion*	following/not following*	repeat/original*
	open/closed*	fact/opinion*	following/not following*	repeat/original*
	open/closed*	fact/opinion*	following/not following*	repeat/original*
	open/closed*	fact/opinion*	following/not following*	repeat/original*
	open/closed*	fact/opinion*	following/not following*	repeat/original*
	open/closed*	fact/opinion*	following/not following*	repeat/original*
	open/closed*	fact/opinion*	following/not following*	repeat/original*
	open/closed*	fact/opinion*	following/not following*	repeat/original*
	open/closed*	fact/opinion*	following/not following*	repeat/original*
	open/closed*	fact/opinion*	following/not following*	repeat/original*
	open/closed*	fact/opinion*	following/not following*	repeat/original*
	open/closed*	fact/opinion*	following/not following*	repeat/original*

* Delete as appropriate

English Attainment Target 1:
Speaking and Listening

Name:
Date of birth:
Home languages:

Talking in a group

➡ Does she or he play with other children, talking to them appropriately?

➡ Will she or he create a role in the home corner, appropriate to the context? For example, if it is set out as a café, will she or he act as a customer or a waiter?

➡ Does she or he sometimes tell a favourite story to a group of friends?

➡ Will she or he make suggestions for what to do next in an activity such as a board game, in making a model, or in a practical mathematics activity?

1a Participate as speakers and listeners in group activities, including imaginative play.

Talking in a group (continued)

➡ Will she or he work with a small group of children preparing a story or a play?

➡ Will she or he work with other children in making a model, suggesting what might be done next?

➡ Does she or he take on roles in semi-structured play, not only in the home corner?

➡ Does she or he talk with other children about aspects of her or his work in class – what to do in a mathematical activity, for example?

2a Participate as speakers and listeners in a group engaged in a given task.

➡ Does she or he listen to other children in a small group discussion?

➡ Does she or he make comments and contributions relevant to the subject matter in a small group discussion with other children?

Child profile record sheets, page 165

Talking in a group (continued)

➡ Does she or he listen to an respond to informal discussions with adults other than the teacher or other usual workers in school?

▼

Level 3: no statement of attainment given.

➡ Does she or he listen with patience and understanding to other children's comments in a small group discussion?

➡ Does she or he base what she or he says on what other speakers have said, responding to their points, rather than acting in relative isolation?

➡ Does she or he listen well to adults other than the teacher and follow their points with some interest?

➡ Does she or he make contributions to discussions, with children and/or adults, that are relevant and reasonably to the point?

▼

4c Take part as speakers and listeners in a group discussion or activity, expressing a personal view and commenting constructively on what is being discussed or experienced.

Talking in a group (continued)

➡ Does she or he develop an argument in a discussion, referring directly to the views expressed by others and responding to them?

➡ Does she or he use evidence, indirect or from personal experience, in making a point in a discussion?

➡ Does she or he marshall her or his ideas into a sequence, speaking with precision and point, to effectively continue a debate?

➡ Does she or he discuss ideas with others in a courteous fashion, if necessary disagreeing with the views of others, but respecting their point of view?

▼

5b Contribute to and respond constructively in discussion, including the development of ideas; advocate and justify a point of view.

Listening and responding to stories

➡ Does she or he listen to short stories, following the main character and situation?

➡ Is she or he able to retell a simple story in her or his own words, picking out a favourite incident?

Child profile record sheets, page 165

Listening and responding to stories (continued)

➡ Can she or he draw a picture that illustrates an incident that she or he found interesting in a story or poem?

➡ Does she or he ask questions about the stories that are read to her or him?

▼

1b Listen attentively, and respond, to stories and poems.

➡ Does she or he identify characters that she or he likes or dislikes in a story, and describe what she or he likes about them?

➡ Does she or he select stories that they have heard before, either asking that they be retold, or making comments that indicate reasons for liking (or disliking) the book?

▼

2c Listen attentively to stories and poems, and talk about them.

➡ Does she or he listen to longer stories being told, either directly by the teacher or from a recording?

➡ Does she or he listen to the teacher or other adults describing a factual incident or event, listening with patience and attention?

Child profile record sheets, page 165

Listening and responding to stories (continued)

➡ Will she or he respond to a story or an account that she or he has heard, expressing interest, asking questions, or otherwise showing that she or he has followed the account?

▼

3c Listen with an increased span of concentration to other children and adults, asking and responding to questions and commenting on what has been said.

Taking messages

➡ Can she or he listen to a simple message, with no more than two parts or elements, and retell this accurately to a teacher or adult?

➡ Can she or he, in role-playing or semi-structured drama, pass on information in role to another person in the drama?

➡ Can she or he take a simple telephone message and pass it on to another person?

▼

3b Convey accurately a simple message.

➡ Can she or he take a more complex message, with more than two parts or elements, and pass it on accurately?

Taking messages (continued)

➡ Can she or he describe a simple event that she or he has taken part in?

➡ Can she or he explain how she or he made a model?

▼

Level 4: no statement of attainment given.

➡ Can she or he take a more complex message, with more than two parts or elements, and pass it on accurately, adding her or his own commentary on the message or the originator of the message, making clear which is the original message and which is comment?

➡ Can she or he give an account of something that she or he has seen, for example, an accident or other incident?

➡ Can she or he explain how something has been lost, describing its appearance?

▼

5c Use language to convey information and ideas effectively in a straightforward situation.

Responding to and giving instructions

➡ Can she or he follow a simple instruction given by the teacher that includes two consecutive instructions?

➡ Does she or he ask what she or he should do next within any particular context?

1c Respond appropriately to simple instructions given by a teacher.

➡ Can she or he follow instructions given by the teacher that include at least three consecutive actions, without needing them repeated part of the way through the task?

➡ Can she or he tell another child how to perform some simple activity that involves at least two consecutive stages?

2e Respond appropriately to a range of more complex instructions given by a teacher, and give simple instructions.

➡ Can she or he give another child exact instructions, with no major ambiguities, about how to carry out a task that involves at least three consecutive stages?

Responding to and giving instructions (continued)

➡ Can she or he follow a series of oral instructions, questioning where appropriate the validity of particular instructions?

➡ Can she or he work effectively in planning an activity within a group, helping to allocate tasks and following tasks it is agreed that she or he carry out?

▼

3d Give, receive and follow accurately, precise instructions when pursuing a task individually or as a member of a group.

Describing and giving an account

➡ Can she or he tell the teacher (or another child) about something that has happened to her or him, including at least three important points, though not necessarily in sequence, and not necessarily giving all the information needed to fully follow the account?

➡ Can she or he describe a story or incident that she or he has seen on television or read about in a book?

▼

2b Describe an event, real or imagined, to the teacher or another pupil.

Describing and giving an account (continued)

➡ Can she or he tell the teacher (or another child) about something that has happened to her or him, including all the important points in the correct sequences?

➡ Can she or he tell a story with a distinct beginning, middle and end?

➡ Can she or he describe an experiment in science, or designing and making something in technology, including the basic relevant information in order?

▼

3a Relate real or imaginary events in a connected narrative which conveys meaning to a group of pupils, the teacher or another known adult.

➡ Can she or he make a report, including all the essential detail as well as several other descriptive details, on the progress of a scientific experiment she or he has been undertaking?

➡ Can she or he give the class or a group an explanation of the planning and progress of an activity being organised by a small group of which she or he is a member, for example, a mini-enterprise activity?

▼

4a Give a detailed oral account of an event, or something that has been learned in the classroom, or explain with reasons why a particular course of action has been taken.

Describing and giving an account (continued)

➥ Can she or he explain to the class how a model was made, giving a clear and full account, including interesting detail about important elements, such as why particular materials were chosen, and why it was designed in the way that it was?

➥ Can she or he give a detailed account of some personal event – a holiday, for example – that is structured and matches the interest and response of the audience?

▼

5a Give a well organised and sustained account of an event, a personal experience or an activity.

Making a presentation

(*NB* These sorts of activities arise naturally out of 'describing and giving an account' in the previous strand.)

➥ Can she or he, alone or as part of a group, describe something in detail that the group has done?

➥ Can she or he give the class or a group a small presentation on the progress of an activity?

➥ Can she or he make an effective oral contribution to an assembly for the school that the class have prepared?

▼

4d Participate in a presentation.

Making a presentation (continued)

➡ Can she or he help plan and participate in a presentation of an event such as a news report for an audience, perhaps of children in another class?

➡ Can she or he take part in an improvised play or presentation for other children?

▼

5d Contribute to the planning of, and participate in, a group presentation.

Answering and asking questions

➡ Does she or he talk with the teacher about activities, asking appropriate questions?

➡ Does she or he listen to what is said by the teacher about activities in class, responding to what is said?

➡ Does she or he answer questions (not necessarily correctly) when asked?

▼

2d Talk with the teacher, listen, and ask and answer questions.

Child profile record sheets, page 165

Answering and asking questions (continued)

➟ Can she or he listen to a story for a length of time, and respond by offering a comment, a summary or questions on the plot, characters and so on?

➟ Can she or he listen to a radio programme or to a topic on tape, and then discuss what was said, with another child or the teacher?

➟ Can she or he listen to other children's views, asking them appropriate questions and answering their points in turn?

▼

3c Listen with an increased span of concentration to other children and adults, asking and responding to questions and commenting on what has been said.

➟ Can she or he help interview an adult other than a teacher, devising and asking appropriate questions in response to earlier answers?

➟ Can she or he help other children in an activity, by asking them appropriate questions and by answering their questions?

▼

4b Ask and respond to questions in a range of situations with increased confidence.